1910s

Decades of the 20th Century
Décadas del siglo XX
Decadi del XX secolo

gettyimages

1910s

Decades of the 20th Century
Décadas del siglo XX
Decadi del XX secolo

Nick Yapp

KÖNEMANN

This book was produced by Getty Images
Unique House, 21–31 Woodfield Road, London W9 2BA

For KÖNEMANN:
Managing editor: Sally Bald
Project editors: Lucile Bas, Meike Hilbring

For Getty Images: Editor: Richard Collins
Art director: Michael Rand   Proof reader: Elisabeth Ihre
Design: B+B   Editorial assistance: Tom Worsley
Picture editor: Ali Khoja   Special thanks: Tea McAleer

© 2004 for the trilingual edition in English, Spanish and Italian:
Tandem Verlag GmbH
KÖNEMANN is a trademark and an imprint of Tandem Verlag GmbH
Spanish translation: Carlos Chacón Zabalza for LocTeam, S. L., Barcelona
Italian translation: Chiara Bombardi for LocTeam, S. L., Barcelona
Text editing and typesetting: LocTeam, S. L., Barcelona

Printed in China

ISBN 3-8331-1146-1

10 9 8 7 6 5 4 3
X IX VIII VII VI V IV III II I

Frontispiece: Three and a half years into the war, Captain and newly-promoted
Mrs Dunville duck under an arch of Lewis guns as they leave the church after their
wedding in April 1918.

Frontispicio: Después de tres años y medio de guerra, el capitán Dunville y su
flamante esposa pasan bajo el arco de honor de fusiles Lewis al abandonar la iglesia
tras su ceremonia nupcial, abril de 1918.

Frontespizio: Nell'aprile 1918, dopo tre anni e mezzo di guerra, il capitano Dunville
e la sua giovane sposa lasciano la chiesa dove si sono appena sposati passando sotto
un arco di fucili Lewis.

Contents / Contenido / Sommario

Introduction

The decade from 1910 to 1919 witnessed the troubled teenage years of the 20th century. They were years of protest, aggression, disappointment, *angst* and bitter disillusion. The hopes that the new century had brought a decade earlier were mown down in a fusillade of wars, revolutions, strikes and armed insurrections culminating, between 1914 and 1918, in the mass slaughter of the First World War.

Blood stained much of the world – Mexico, Ireland, the Middle East, China, India, Africa, South America and, above all, Europe. Incompetent kings and bewildered statesmen were assassinated – an increasingly easy task with modern weapons. Democratic governments reeled under attacks from women and workers, for the dual spectres of militant suffragettes and organised labour were more than most governments could tolerate. In 1911 Britain was crippled by a series of strikes involving seamen, dockers, miners and railwaymen. At much the same time, the French Ministry of the Interior prepared its 'carnet B', a list of the trade unionists to be arrested in the event of war. A year later the German army was called out to deal with strikers in Hamburg and the Ruhr. On the eve of the First World War, Italy ground to a halt in the national strike of 'Red Week'.

Through it all shone the brilliance of human achievement. It was a decade that began with Stravinsky's *Firebird* and Bertrand Russell's *Principia Mathematica*, and ended with the foundation of the Bauhaus and the first visit to Europe of the Original Dixieland Jazz Band. Between these milestones Roland Garros flew across the Mediterranean, and Alcock and Brown crossed the Atlantic. Amundsen beat Scott to the South Pole. Marie Stopes published *Married Love*, and Gandhi led the Indian Independence Movement. Chaplin arrived at the Keystone Film Company in Hollywood, and D W Griffith produced *The Birth of a Nation*.

The last horse-drawn bus disappeared from the streets of London, and the first regular passenger flights between London and Paris were inaugurated. A bold aviator made the world's first parachute jump, and a bold editor published the first copy of *Pravda*. Doctor Harry Plotz discovered a typhus vaccine; Henry Ford set up the world's first assembly line.

For almost the last time, French, German, Italian and Spanish politicians deluded themselves that Europe was the cultural, industrial and financial hub of the world. The ancient order maintained its Ruritanian elegance and atavistic pomp and ceremony. But by 1919 the brave old continent was exhausted. Sooner or later the might of both the United States and the new Union of Soviet Socialist Republics would have to be recognised.

Introducción

La década de 1910 a 1919 fue una época convulsa. Fueron unos años de protesta, agresividad, decepciones, angustia y amargas desilusiones. Las esperanzas que el nuevo siglo había traído consigo la década anterior se vinieron abajo por culpa de las guerras, las revoluciones, las huelgas y las insurrecciones armadas que culminaron, entre 1914 y 1918, con la masacre que supuso la Primera Guerra Mundial.

La sangre tiñó de rojo gran parte del mundo: México, Irlanda, Oriente Próximo, China, India, África, Sudamérica y, sobre todo, Europa. Monarcas incompetentes y desconcertados hombres de Estado fueron asesinados, lo cual resultó increíblemente fácil gracias a las armas modernas. Los Gobiernos democráticos se tambalearon a causa de las reivindicaciones de las mujeres y los obreros, ya que el doble espectro de las sufragistas militantes y los sindicatos constituían una amenaza intolerable para la mayoría de los Gobiernos. En 1911, Gran Bretaña quedó paralizada por una serie de huelgas protagonizadas por marineros, estibadores, mineros y ferroviarios. Por aquel entonces, el ministro del Interior francés preparó su "carné B", una lista de los sindicalistas que debían ser arrestados en caso de guerra. Un año después, el ejército alemán salió a la calle para aplacar a los huelguistas en Hamburgo y en el Ruhr. En vísperas de la Primera Guerra Mundial, Italia quedó paralizada por el movimiento de huelga nacional conocido como "Semana Roja".

Sin embargo, esta década fue también una época de brillantes logros humanos. Comenzó con el *Pájaro de fuego* de Stravinsky y los *Principia Mathematica* de Bertrand Russell, y culminó con la fundación de la Bauhaus y la primera visita a Europa de la Original Dixieland Jazz Band. Entre dichos acontecimientos, Roland Garros atravesó el Mediterráneo por aire y Alcock y Brown realizaron el primer vuelo transatlántico. Amundsen llegó al Polo Sur antes que Scott. Marie Stopes publicó *Married Love* y Gandhi lideró el Movimiento de Independencia Indio. Chaplin llegó a la Keystone Film Company en Hollywood y D. W. Griffith produjo *El nacimiento de una nación*. Los últimos autobuses tirados por caballos desaparecieron de las calles de Londres y comenzaron los vuelos regulares de pasajeros entre Londres y París. Un osado aviador hizo el primer salto en paracaídas del mundo y un atrevido editor publicó el primer ejemplar de *Prawda*. El doctor Harry Plotz descubrió la vacuna del tifus y Henry Ford puso en marcha la primera cadena de montaje del mundo.

Casi por primera vez, los políticos franceses, alemanes, italianos y españoles se crearon la ilusión de que Europa era el centro cultural, industrial y financiero del mundo. El antiguo orden conservó la ilusión de un reino imaginario con los fastos y las pompas de antaño. Pero en 1919 el viejo continente estaba exhausto. Tarde o temprano habría que reconocer el poder de Estados Unidos y de la nueva Unión de Repúblicas Socialistas Soviéticas.

Introduzione

Gli anni tra il 1910 e il 1919 furono anni inquieti per il XX secolo ancora adolescente: anni di proteste, violenza, delusione, angoscia esistenziale e amara disillusione. Le speranze generate un decennio prima dalla nascita del nuovo secolo furono fatte a pezzi da una serie di guerre, rivoluzioni, scioperi e insurrezioni armate che culminò, tra il 1914 e il 1918, nel massacro della Prima guerra mondiale.

Il mondo fu macchiato di sangue quasi per intero: il Messico, l'Irlanda, il Medio Oriente, la Cina, l'India, l'Africa, l'America del Sud e soprattutto l'Europa. Le armi moderne permisero di assassinare con la stessa facilità tanto sovrani incompetenti quanto increduli uomini di stato. Molti governi democratici crollarono sotto il peso delle rivendicazioni delle suffragiste e del movimento operaio, che assieme rappresentavano una minaccia troppo grande per la maggior parte di essi. Nel 1911 la Gran Bretagna fu letteralmente paralizzata da una catena di scioperi che coinvolsero marinai, portuali, minatori e ferrovieri. Quasi contemporaneamente, il ministro degli Interni francese redigeva il "carnet B", una lista di sindacalisti da arrestare in caso di guerra. Un anno dopo, l'esercito tedesco fu chiamato a soffocare gli scioperi di Amburgo e della Ruhr. Alla vigilia della Prima guerra mondiale l'Italia intera si fermò per uno sciopero su scala nazionale passato alla storia come la "settimana rossa".

Malgrado tutto ciò, il decennio non fu privo di brillanti conquiste da parte dell'umanità. Ebbe inizio con l'*Uccello di fuoco* di Stravinsky e i *Principia Mathematica* di Bertrand Russell e terminò con la creazione del movimento Bauhaus e la prima tournée europea dell'Original Dixieland Jazz Band. Roland Garros portò a termine la traversata aerea del Mediterraneo, Alcock e Brown attraversarono l'Atlantico e Amundsen arrivò al Polo Sud prima di Scott. Marie Stopes pubblicò *Married Love* mentre Gandhi guidava il movimento d'indipendenza indiana. Chaplin debuttò a Hollywood con la Keystone Film Company e D.W. Griffith realizzò *Nascita di una nazione*. L'ultimo autobus trainato da cavalli scomparve dalle strade londinesi e furono inaugurati i primi voli di linea tra Londra e Parigi. Un aviatore temerario eseguì il primo salto col paracadute mentre un editore coraggioso pubblicava la prima edizione della *Pravda*. Il Dott. Harry Plotz scoprì il vaccino contro il tifo e Henry Ford inventò la prima catena di montaggio del mondo. Per l'ultima volta o quasi i politici francesi, tedeschi, italiani e spagnoli coltivarono l'illusione che l'Europa fosse il centro culturale, industriale e finanziario del mondo. Il vecchio ordine manteneva fasti e pompe appartenenti a un'epoca ormai tramontata. Ma nel 1919 il vecchio continente stava esaurendo le sue risorse. Presto o tardi, avrebbe dovuto riconoscere la potenza degli Stati Uniti e della neonata Unione delle Repubbliche Socialiste Sovietiche.

1. Conflict
Conflictos
Conflitti

In the early days of Dr Sun Yat-sen's government in China, a crowd gathers to view the decapitated bodies of robbers. The old Manchu ways of summary justice remained.

El régimen de Sun Yat-sen da sus primeros pasos en China y una multitud se agolpa para ver los cuerpos decapitados de unos ladrones. Por aquel entonces subsistían los viejos métodos manchús de justicia sumaria.

Nei primi giorni del governo di Sun Yat-sen in Cina, una folla si raduna attorno ai corpi decapitati dei ladri. Sussistono ancora i metodi sommari della giustizia manchù.

1. Conflict
Conflictos
Conflitti

The whole world lost its temper. For centuries the poor, hungry and oppressed masses had endured hardship and deprivation with the tolerance of despair. European powers had enslaved one third of the world and exploited as much again. Women had accepted the status of second-class citizens in even the most civilised of societies. Labour had kowtowed to bosses who ranged from the considerate to the cruel. The status quo had rarely been seriously challenged. Now came wars of independence, national strikes, protests by women. From all quarters there were strident demands for change and reform. There was a new spirit abroad. Worse, there was a new spirit at home.

Old empires tried to hit back, but most were unfit for the struggle. The Ottoman Empire reeled under attack by the Balkan League. The Chinese Empire disintegrated in the bloodbath of civil conflict. The Russian and Austro-Hungarian empires shrivelled and died. The British Empire somehow held on, though the cost of protecting and, at the same time, repressing its increasingly discontented colonies was beginning to prove too much.

The world was about to explode.

El mundo entero perdió los estribos. Durante siglos, las masas pobres, hambrientas y oprimidas habían aguantado muchas privaciones a causa de la desesperación. Las potencias europeas habían esclavizado a una tercera parte del mundo y habían explotado a otro tercio. Las mujeres habían aceptado la condición de ciudadanos de segunda incluso en las sociedades más civilizadas. Los obreros se habían doblegado ante los patronos, quienes podían ser considerados o crueles. El *statu quo* nunca había sido realmente desafiado. Había llegado la hora de las guerras de independencia, las huelgas nacionales y las protestas de las mujeres. De todos los rincones surgían violentas reivindicaciones de cambios y reformas.

Reinaba un nuevo espíritu en todo el mundo. Y, lo que era peor, ese nuevo espíritu era claramente patente en casa.

Los antiguos imperios trataron de contraatacar. El imperio otomano se tambaleó a causa de los ataques de la Liga Balcánica. El imperio chino se desintegró tras el baño de sangre causado por la guerra civil. Los imperios ruso y austrohúngaro se marchitaron y acabaron desapareciendo. El imperio británico resistía como podía aunque el coste de proteger a sus colonias y, al mismo tiempo, reprimir el creciente descontento que reinaba en ellas empezaba a ser excesivo.

El mundo entero estaba a punto de explotar.

Il mondo intero entrò in collera. Per secoli le masse povere, affamate e oppresse, avevano sopportato qualsiasi prova e privazione con la forza della disperazione. Le potenze europee avevano ridotto in schiavitù un terzo della popolazione del pianeta e sfruttato un altro terzo di essa. Le donne avevano accettato lo status di cittadini di seconda classe, anche in seno alle società più evolute. Gli operai si erano inchinati di fronte ai padroni più crudeli. Lo status quo era stato raramente messo in discussione. Di colpo fu il momento delle guerre d'indipendenza, degli scioperi nazionali, delle manifestazioni femministe. Violente richieste di cambiamenti e riforme provenivano da ogni dove. All'estero si respirava già un'aria diversa. E, quel che è peggio, anche a casa si cominciava a percepire la stessa aria.

I vecchi imperi tentarono di contrattaccare, ma la maggior parte di essi non era preparata per il confronto. L'Impero ottomano vacillò sotto il peso dell'Intesa balcanica. L'Impero cinese si disintegrò in un bagno di sangue causato dalla guerra civile. Gli imperi russo e austro-ungarico si consumarono fino a spegnersi. L'Impero britannico resisteva come poteva, anche se il costo della protezione e al tempo stesso repressione delle sue colonie sempre più scontente cominciava ad essere troppo elevato.

Il mondo stava per esplodere.

Winston Churchill – as Home Secretary (in top hat, on left of main group) – with armed police and members of the Scots Guards at the Sidney Street siege, Stepney, London, 3 January 1911. They were besieging a house of anarchists.

Winston Churchill –como ministro de Interior (con sombrero alto, a la izquierda del grupo principal)– con policías y miembros de la Guardia Escocesa armados sitian una casa ocupada por anarquistas en Sidney Street, en el barrio de Stepney, Londres, el 3 de enero de 1911.

L'allora Ministro degli Interni Winston Churchill (a sinistra del gruppo principale, con un cappello a cilindro) assieme a poliziotti e membri della Guardia scozzese durante l'assedio di una casa occupata da anarchici in Sidney Street, nel quartiere londinese di Stepney, il 3 gennaio 1911.

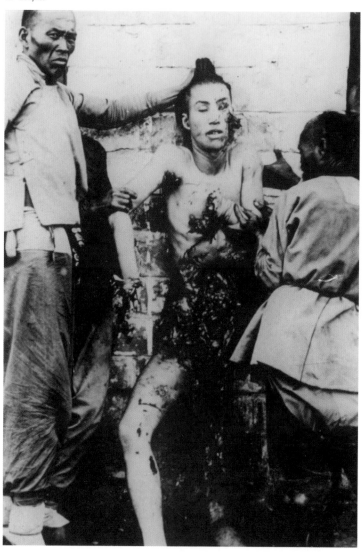

The victim of a bomb explosion (possibly his own bomb) is exhibited during the revolution in China, 1912.

La víctima de la explosión de una bomba (tal vez, su propia bomba) es mostrada al público durante la revolución de China, en 1912.

La vittima dell'esplosione di una bomba (forse la sua) viene mostrata al pubblico durante la rivoluzione cinese, nel 1912.

Two foreigners gaze at a headless body in a city street in China, 1912. The revolution to overthrow Manchu rule boiled over into horrendous violence after the death of the Dowager Empress in 1908.

Dos extranjeros contemplan un cadáver decapitado en plena calle de una ciudad china, en 1912. La revolución para derrocar el régimen manchú generó una espiral de violencia inenarrable tras la muerte de la emperatriz viuda en 1908.

Due stranieri osservano un corpo decapitato in una strada di una città cinese, nel 1912. La rivoluzione volta a rovesciare il governo manchù sfociò in una terribile ondata di violenza dopo la morte della vedova dell'imperatore nel 1908.

The execution of a Chinese revolutionary, 1912. The term 'revolutionary' was widely construed to include anyone who opposed or criticised local, as well as national, authority. Scenes like this were common in town and country.

Ejecución de un revolucionario chino, en 1912. El término "revolucionario" era lo suficientemente vago como para incluir a todos los opositores o críticos de las autoridades locales y nacionales. Escenas como esta eran habituales tanto en las ciudades como en el campo.

Esecuzione di un rivoluzionario cinese nel 1912. Il termine "rivoluzionario" includeva chiunque si opponesse o criticasse l'autorità, sia locale che nazionale. Scene simili a questa erano all'ordine del giorno in città e in campagna.

By 1911 many supporters of the Old Order in China believed that a bloodbath was inevitable. This victim may have been pro- or anti-revolution. For many, it was simply a matter of being in the wrong place at the wrong time.

En 1911, muchos partidarios del antiguo régimen chino consideraban inevitable un baño de sangre. Resulta difícil saber si esta víctima estaba a favor o en contra de la revolución. Por desgracia, muchas veces era suficiente con estar en el lugar equivocado en el momento menos oportuno.

Nel 1911 molti difensori del vecchio regime cinese ritenevano che un bagno di sangue fosse ormai inevitabile. È difficile sapere se questa vittima fosse pro o contro la rivoluzione. Spesso si trattava semplicemente di trovarsi al posto sbagliato nel momento sbagliato.

Unionists parade outside the City Hall, Belfast, 28 September 1912. They
were queueing to sign Edward Carson's Solemn League and Covenant, which
promised an armed struggle to fight against Home Rule for Ireland.

Los unionistas se manifiestan ante el Ayuntamiento de Belfast, el 28 de septiembre
de 1912. Hacían cola para firmar el Covenant y la Liga Solemne de Edward Carson,
que prometían el combate armado para luchar contra la aplicación de la Home Rule
(la concesión de la autonomía política) en Irlanda.

Sfilata di Unionisti davanti alla City Hall di Belfast, il 28 settembre 1912. Fanno la
coda per firmare la Solemn League and Covenant di Edward Carson che promette
di combattere con le armi la Home Rule, il diritto all'autodeterminazione dell'Irlanda.

Sir Edward Carson in full flow, 1912. The introduction of the third Home Rule Bill to the House of Commons in 1912 infuriated the Ulster Unionists and led to the organisation by Carson of the Ulster Defence Volunteers.

Sir Edward Carson en pleno discurso, en 1912. La presentación de una tercera Home Rule Bill ante la cámara del Parlamento en 1912 enfureció a los unionistas del Ulster y llevó a Carson a crear los Voluntarios del Ulster.

Discorso di Sir Edward Carson, nel 1912. La presentazione alla Camera dei Comuni della terza legge sull'Home Rule nel 1912 fece infuriare gli Unionisti dell'Ulster e spinse Carson a organizzare l'Ulster Defence Volunteers.

On the brink of war. Crowds gather for the funeral of one of the victims shot by the
King's Own Scottish Borderers during what became known as the Bachelor's Walk
massacre, Dublin, 29 July 1914.

Al borde de la guerra. Una gran multitud acude al entierro de una de las víctimas
asesinadas por la Guardia Real Escocesa, tragedia que se conoció como la Masacre
de Bachelor's Walk, Dublín, el 29 de julio de 1914.

Sull'orlo della guerra. Una folla immensa si è riunita per il funerale di una delle vittime
uccise dalla Guardia reale scozzese in occasione di quello che verrà chiamato in seguito
il massacro di Bachelor's Walk, Dublino, 29 luglio 1914.

A Scottish Borderer closes the door to the regiment's barracks after the massacre, 28 July 1914. Four civilians were killed and thirty-eight injured after soldiers failed to capture Irish Volunteers involved in gun-running at Howth.

Un soldado de la Guardia Escocesa cierra la puerta del cuartel del regimiento tras la masacre, el 28 de julio de 1914. Cuatro civiles resultaron muertos y treinta y ocho heridos cuando los soldados trataban en vano de capturar a los Voluntarios Irlandeses implicados en operaciones de tráfico de armas en Howth.

Un soldato della Guardia scozzese chiude la porta della caserma del reggimento dopo il massacro del 28 luglio 1914. Quattro civili furono uccisi e 38 feriti mentre i soldati tentavano invano di catturare i "Volontari irlandesi" responsabili di avere organizzato un traffico d'armi a Howth.

In a scene foreshadowing revolution on the streets of St Petersburg, police charge Irish strikers on the streets of Dublin, August 1913. One striker was killed and many injured.

La imagen, que muestra a la policía irlandesa cargando contra los huelguistas en una calle de Dublín en agosto de 1913, es un anticipo de lo que ocurriría en San Petersburgo en plena revolución. Un huelguista resultó muerto y varios, heridos.

In uno scenario che anticipa lo scoppio della rivoluzione nelle strade di San Pietroburgo, la polizia carica un gruppo di scioperanti irlandesi, agosto 1913. Un manifestante viene ucciso e molti altri feriti.

Three years after escaping execution in the aftermath of the Easter Rising, Eamon de Valera addresses a meeting in Los Angeles, December 1919. He was touring the United States as president of the Dail Eireann.

Tres años después de escapar de la ejecución tras el Levantamiento de Pascua, Eamon de Valera celebra un mitin en Los Ángeles, en diciembre de 1919. Recorrió Estados Unidos como presidente de la Dail Eireann, cámara baja del Parlamento irlandés.

Tre anni dopo essere sfuggito all'esecuzione in seguito all'insurrezione di Pasqua, Eamon de Valera tiene un discorso a Los Angeles nel dicembre del 1919, in qualità di presidente del Dail Eireann, il parlamento irlandese.

The General Post Office, Sackville Street, Dublin, April 1916. It was here that the proclamation of the Irish Republic began the Easter Rising.

La oficina central de correos de Dublín en Sackville Street, en abril de 1916. Fue aquí donde la proclamación de la República irlandesa desencadenó el Levantamiento de Pascua.

La posta centrale di Sackville Street a Dublino, aprile 1916. È qui che la proclamazione della Repubblica irlandese dà inizio all'insurrezione di Pasqua.

British troops in action near the Dublin quays during the Easter Rising, April 1916. One hundred British soldiers and 450 Irish fighters were killed.

Tropas británicas en acción cerca del muelle de Dublín durante el Levantamiento de Pascua, en abril de 1916. Cien soldados británicos y 450 combatientes irlandeses resultaron muertos.

Soldati britannici in azione vicino al porto di Dublino durante l'insurrezione di Pasqua, aprile 1916. Cento soldati britannici e 450 combattenti irlandesi furono uccisi.

The charred shell of the General Post Office, Dublin, Easter 1916.
It was the focal point of the fighting in what many regard as the first
modern rising against colonial rule.

Bóveda calcinada de la oficina central de correos de Dublín, Semana
Santa de 1916. Punto neurálgico de los combates en lo que fue, para
muchos, el primer levantamiento moderno contra la autoridad colonial.

La carcassa della posta centrale di Dublino, Pasqua 1916. Fu qui che
si concentrarono i combattimenti di quella che molti considerano la
prima rivolta moderna contro il potere coloniale.

Children in a poor area of Dublin collect firewood from the piles of rubble created by fighting during the Easter Rising. In general, the population of Dublin responded to the Rising with determined indifference.

Niños de un barrio pobre de Dublín recogen leña entre los escombros provocados por el Levantamiento de Pascua. En general, la población de Dublín vivió la insurrección con absoluta indiferencia.

Dei bambini di un quartiere povero di Dublino raccolgono legna per il fuoco tra le rovine causate dai combattimenti durante l'insurrezione di Pasqua. In generale, la popolazione di Dublino rispose all'insurrezione con ostinata indifferenza.

British muscles, 1919. The sign reads 'It is absolutely forbidden to cross this border into Afghan territory'. The British were there to prop up the failing White Russian cause after the Revolution of 1917.

Fuerzas británicas, 1919. La pancarta reza: "Queda absolutamente prohibido cruzar esta frontera y entrar en territorio afgano". Los británicos estaban allí para apoyar la débil causa de los rusos blancos tras la revolución de 1917.

Forze britanniche, 1919. Il pannello recita "È severamente proibito attraversare la frontiera ed entrare in territorio afgano". I britannici difendevano la causa vacillante dei Russi bianchi dopo la rivoluzione del 1917.

Afghanistan muzzles, 1910. A group of tribesmen pose for the camera somewhere near the Khyber Pass. At the time, the area was unusually and disconcertingly quiet.

Combatientes afganos, 1910. Varios miembros de una tribu posan para la cámara cerca del paso de Khyber. Por aquel entonces, la región vivía una paz inusual y desconcertante.

Tiratori afgani, 1910. I membri di una tribù si fanno ritrarre da qualche parte vicino al passo di Khyber. All'epoca la regione era sorprendentemente calma.

Members of General Francisco 'Pancho' Villa's rebel army enter the city of Sinaltua
shortly after its capture during the Mexican Revolutionary War, November 1913.
The war lasted until the 1920s.

Miembros del ejército rebelde del General Francisco "Pancho" Villa entran en la ciudad
de Sinaltua poco después de hacerse con el control de la misma durante la Revolución
Mexicana, en noviembre de 1913. La guerra duró hasta la década de 1920.

Membri dell'esercito ribelle del generale Francisco "Pancho" Villa entrano a Sinaltua
poco dopo la sua presa durante la rivoluzione messicana, nel novembre del 1913.
La guerra durò fino agli anni Venti.

Casualties of war lie on the streets of Mexico City. After the capture of Juárez in November 1913, Villa led his men on to the capital to take on the army of General Huerta, the *de facto* ruler of Mexico.

Varias víctimas de la guerra yacen en las calles de México. Tras la captura de Juárez en noviembre de 1913, Villa y sus hombres se dirigieron a la capital para luchar contra el ejército del General Huerta, que era el jefe de Estado de facto de México.

Vittime della guerra giacciono per le strade di Città del Messico. Dopo la presa di Juárez nel novembre del 1913, Villa e i suoi uomini si dressero verso la capitale, per affrontare l'esercito del Generale Huerta, il capo di stato *de facto* del Messico.

Emiliano Zapata,
leader of the rebels
in southern Mexico,
1915. Zapata was
part brigand, part
general.

Emiliano Zapata,
líder de los rebeldes
del sur de México,
en 1915. Zapata
era medio forajido
y medio general.

Emiliano Zapata,
il leader dei ribelli
del sud del Messico,
nel 1915. Zapata
era mezzo brigante,
mezzo generale.

In the early days of the war, Pancho Villa leads a section of the rebel army, January 1911. Villa's fugitive life began at the age of 16 and ended twenty-nine years later in his death in a revenge killing.

A principios de la guerra, Pancho Villa encabeza una sección del ejército rebelde, en enero de 1911. La vida de Villa como fugitivo comenzó a los 16 años y finalizó 29 años después cuando fue asesinado en un acto de represalia.

Nel gennaio del 1911, all'inizio della guerra, Pancho Villa comanda una sezione dell'esercito ribelle. La vita di fuggitivo di Villa ebbe inizio a 16 anni e si concluse 29 anni dopo, quando venne ucciso in un atto di rappresaglia.

The suffragette Emily Davison is killed as she throws herself under the King's horse at the Epsom Derby, 4 June 1913.

La sufragista Emily Davison murió tras tirarse a los pies del caballo del rey durante el derbi de Epsom, el 4 de junio de 1913.

La suffragista Emily Davison muore buttandosi sotto il cavallo del re in occasione del Derby di Epsom, 4 giugno 1913.

A militant suffragette is arrested during a day of disturbance in central London, 21 May 1914.

Arresto de una militante sufragista durante un día de altercados en el centro de Londres, el 21 de mayo de 1914.

Una suffragista militante viene arrestata durante una protesta nel centro di Londra, 21 maggio 1914.

On the same day, the burly arms of the law remove Emmeline Pankhurst from the vicinity of Buckingham Palace. As active co-founder of the Women's Social and Political Union, she was used to being arrested.

El mismo día, el largo brazo de la ley aleja a Emmeline Pankhurst de las proximidades de Buckingham Palace. Como cofundadora activa de la Unión Social y Política de las Mujeres, estaba acostumbrada a los arrestos.

Lo stesso giorno, le forti braccia della polizia in borghese prelevano Emmeline Pankhurst non lontano da Buckingham Palace. Cofondatrice della Women's Social and Political Union, era ormai abituata a essere arrestata.

A group of Austrians demonstrate for women's rights in Vienna,
19 March 1911. The slogan on the placard reads: 'Equal duties,
equal rights'. Austrian women were enfranchised in 1918.

Un grupo de austriacas se manifiesta en defensa de los derechos de
la mujer en Viena, el 19 de marzo de 1911. El eslogan de la pancarta
reza: "A igualdad de deberes, igualdad de derechos". En 1918 se
reconoció el derecho al voto de la mujer en Austria.

Un gruppo di austriache manifestano a favore dei diritti della donna a
Vienna, il 19 marzo 1911. Lo slogan sui cartelli recita: "Doveri uguali,
diritti uguali". Le austriache ricevettero il diritto di voto nel 1918.

Members of the National American Woman Suffrage Association parade in New York, 3 May 1913. Their persistence paid off in August 1920 with the ratification of the Nineteenth Amendment, giving American women the franchise on an equal basis with men. Thereafter the NAWSA ceased to exist.

Desfile de miembros de la National American Women Suffrage Association en Nueva York, el 3 de mayo de 1913. Su persistencia se vio premiada en agosto de 1920 con la ratificación de la Decimonovena Enmienda que reconocía el derecho al voto de la mujer en las mismas condiciones que el hombre. Tras la victoria, la NAWSA dejó de existir.

Membri della National American Woman Suffrage Association sfilano a New York il 3 maggio 1913. La loro perseveranza diede i suoi frutti nell'agosto del 1920 con la ratifica del XIX emendamento che accorda alle donne americane il diritto di voto. Dopo questa vittoria, la NAWSA si sciolse.

Female fervour.
An impassioned and
impromptu speech
by an American
suffragette in a
New York street,
1912.

Fervor femenino.
Una sufragista
estadounidense
pronuncia un
discurso apasionado
e improvisado en
una calle de Nueva
York, en 1912.

Fervore femminile.
Una suffragista
americana tiene
un discorso
appassionato e
improvvisato in una
strada di New York,
nel 1912.

Male mockery. A group of men destroy a banner taken from a suffragette picket line outside the White House, Washington DC, 1912. There were many men who objected to women smoking and drinking, let alone voting.

Burla masculina. Un grupo de hombres destruye un cartel sustraído a un piquete de huelga de sufragistas frente a la Casa Blanca en Washington, D. C., en 1912. Muchos hombres se oponían a que las mujeres fumaran y bebieran, ¡y solo faltaba que pudieran votar!

Beffa maschile. Degli uomini fanno a pezzi uno striscione strappato a un picchetto di suffragiste davanti alla Casa Bianca, Washington D.C., nel 1912. Molti uomini non accettavano che le donne fumassero, bevessero e soprattutto votassero.

Miners in South Wales lubricate their dusty throats with pints of bitter and discuss the start of a major strike, 27 February 1912. Within five days, over a million of their colleagues had withdrawn their labour.

Mineros del sur de Gales apagan su sed con unas pintas de cerveza mientras debaten el comienzo de una gran huelga, el 27 de febrero de 1912. Cinco días después, más de un millón de mineros dejaban de trabajar.

Minatori del Galles del sud calmano la sete con una pinta di birra e discutono dell'inizio di un grande sciopero, 27 febbraio 1912. Cinque giorni più tardi, più di un milione di loro colleghi avrebbero smesso di lavorare.

A couple of hundred miles away, women mine workers stage a sit-down protest on a pile of coal at a mine near Wigan, Lancashire. Three weeks later, the British Government granted coal workers a minimum wage.

A unos cientos de kilómetros de allí, empleadas de una mina cercana a Wigan (Lancashire) protagonizaban una huelga sentadas sobre una montaña de carbón. Tres semanas después, el Gobierno británico concedió un salario mínimo a los mineros del carbón.

A poche centinaia di chilometri, delle lavoratrici di una miniera di Wigan (Lancashire) improvvisano uno sciopero su una montagna di carbone. Tre settimane dopo, il governo britannico concedeva un salario minimo ai minatori.

In October 1912, Bulgaria, prime mover of the Balkan League, declared war on the Ottoman Empire. Here a Bulgarian field gun is moved into position during the siege of Adrianople, August 1913.

En octubre de 1912, Bulgaria, padre de la Liga de los Balcanes, declaró la guerra al imperio otomano. En la fotografía, un cañón búlgaro es colocado en posición de tiro durante el sitio de Adrianópolis (Edirne), agosto de 1913.

Nell'ottobre del 1912 la Bulgaria, iniziatrice dell'Intesa balcanica, dichiara guerra all'Impero ottomano. Qui, un cannone bulgaro viene messo in posizione di tiro durante l'assedio di Adrianopoli, nell'agosto del 1913.

Soldiers remove their dead comrades from the battlefield of Adrianople, October 1913. The war was staggering towards its end, leaving a few months of uneasy peace before the tragedy of Sarajevo.

Unos soldados retiran los cuerpos sin vida de sus compañeros en la batalla de Adrianópolis, en octubre de 1913. La guerra tocaba a su fin para dar paso a unos meses de paz incierta antes de la tragedia de Sarajevo.

Dei soldati rimuovono i corpi dei loro compagni morti sul campo di battaglia a Adrianopoli, ottobre 1913. La guerra sta per finire e lasciare il posto a qualche mese di pace incerta prima della tragedia di Sarajevo.

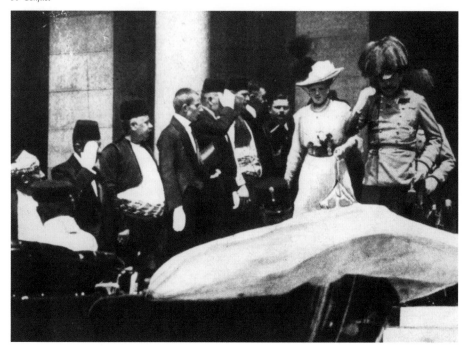

Archduke Franz Ferdinand of Austria and the Duchess Sophia prepare
to leave Sarajevo ahead of schedule on the fateful afternoon of 28 June
1914. An attempt had already been made on their lives.

El archiduque Francisco Fernando de Austria y la duquesa Sofía
abandonan Sarajevo antes de lo previsto aquella fatídica tarde del 28 de
junio de 1914. Ya se había producido un atentado que pretendía acabar
con sus vidas.

L'arciduca Francesco Ferdinando d'Austria e la duchessa Sofia lasciano
Sarajevo prima del previsto nel fatidico pomeriggio del 28 giugno
1914. In precedenza erano già stati vittime di un attentato.

The royal cavalcade sets off for the railway station in Sarajevo. Moments later it took a wrong turning, stopped, and Gavrilo Princip struck.

La comitiva real parte hacia la estación de Sarajevo. Unos momentos después, tras girar por una calle cercana, se detuvo y Gavrilo Princip disparó.

La cavalleria reale si avvia verso la stazione di Sarajevo. Qualche istante più tardi prende la strada sbagliata, deve fermarsi e Gavrilo Princip spara.

Nedeljko Cabrinovic, one of Princip's fellow conspirators, is hustled away by police after his failed attempt at assassinating the Archduke. Princip's successful attempt was made a couple of hours later.

Nedeljko Cabrinovic, uno de los cómplices de Princip, es arrestado por la policía tras su intento de asesinato del archiduque. Unas horas después, Princip no fallaría.

Nedeljko Cabrinovic, uno dei complici di Princip, viene portato via dalla polizia dopo il tentato assassinio dell'arciduca. Qualche ora dopo, Princip riuscirà nel suo intento.

The bloodstained
tunic of the
Archduke is
placed on display.
The spark was
about to set the
world ablaze.

La guerrera
del archiduque
manchada de
sangre es exhibida
al público. Fue la
chispa que prendió
fuego al mundo.

La tunica
macchiata di sangue
dell'arciduca viene
mostrata al
pubblico. È la
scintilla che fa
esplodere il mondo.

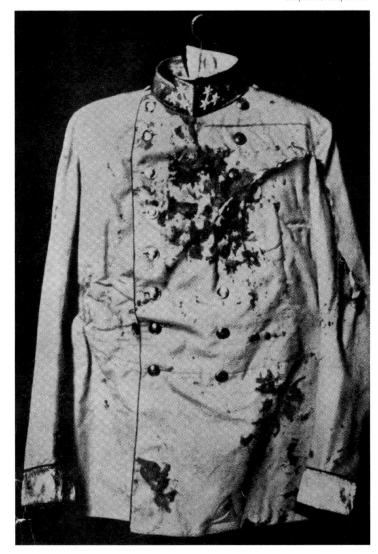

2. The Western Front
El frente occidental
Il fronte occidentale

French soldiers on the battlefield of Verdun, August 1917. For months the fortifications here were the flash point of the Western Front, a deadly test of strength between German and French armies.

Soldados franceses en el campo de batalla de Verdún, en agosto de 1917. Durante meses, las fortificaciones constituyeron el punto neurálgico del frente occidental, una prueba de fuerza mortal para los ejércitos francés y alemán.

Soldati francesi sul campo di battaglia di Verdun, agosto 1917. Per mesi, queste fortificazioni furono il fulcro del fronte occidentale, una prova di forza mortale per gli eserciti francese e tedesco.

2. The Western Front
El frente occidental
Il fronte occidentale

It was all going to be over by Christmas. Everyone said so – the French commanders, the Russian commanders, the British and German commanders. The Kaiser promised his troops, as they prepared to leave Berlin in August 1914, that they would be back 'before the leaves fall from the trees'.

But the war on the Western Front dragged on for 1,559 days, creating seas of mud and fields of slaughter from the Channel to the Swiss border. Men choked to death on poison gas, drowned in flooded shell holes, bled to death from shell and bullet wounds. The sacrifice made by the young and innocent at Ypres, Verdun, the Marne, the Somme, Passchendaele, Cambrai, Arras, Vimy Ridge and a hundred more killing fields was on an unprecedented scale.

Governments, profiteers, churchmen and generals demanded that they fight on. The dreadful doctrine of attrition was invoked to justify the tactics of slaughter: we have more men than the enemy, therefore the sooner all combatants are killed, the sooner we shall emerge as victors.

The grotesque parade marched on.

Todo habría terminado en Navidad. Eso decían todos, tanto los generales franceses, como los rusos, los británicos y los alemanes. El káiser prometió a sus tropas, cuando se preparaban para abandonar Berlín en agosto de 1914, que estarían de vuelta "antes de que cayeran las hojas de los árboles".

Pero la guerra en el frente occidental duró 1.599 días y generó mares de fango y campos de masacre desde el canal de la Mancha hasta la frontera suiza. Los hombres morían asfixiados por el gas del combate, ahogados en boquetes de obuses inundados, desangrados a causa de las heridas de los obuses y las balas. El sacrificio de hombres jóvenes e inocentes en Ypres, Verdún, el Marne, el Somme, Passchendaele, Cambrai, Arras, la cresta de Vimy y cientos de campos más no tenía precedente alguno.

Gobernantes, especuladores, eclesiásticos, generales; todos les pedían que siguieran luchando. Se invocó la espantosa doctrina de la guerra de desgaste para justificar la táctica de la masacre: disponemos de más hombres que el enemigo, por lo tanto, cuanto antes acabemos con nuestros adversarios, antes nos erigiremos en ganadores.

El macabro desfile avanzaba hacia el combate.

Tutto sarebbe finito a Natale. Era quello che dicevano tutti, tanto i generali francesi come quelli russi, britannici o tedeschi. Il "Kaiser" promise alle sue truppe che si apprestavano a lasciare Berlino nell'agosto del 1914 che sarebbero state di ritorno "prima che le foglie cadano dagli alberi".

Ma la guerra sul fronte occidentale si trascinò per 1.559 giorni, generando un mare di fango e morti che andava dalla Manica alla frontiera svizzera. Gli uomini cadevano asfissiati dai gas velenosi, annegati nelle buche allagate scavate dalle granate, dissanguati per le ferite causate da bombe e proiettili. Il sacrificio di giovani innocenti a Ypres, a Verdun, sulla Marna, sulla Somma, a Passchendaele, a Cambrai, a Arras, a Vimy Ridge e su centinaia di altri campi di morte fu senza precedenti.

Governanti, affaristi, ecclesiastici, generali, tutti esigevano che la battaglia continuasse. La terribile dottrina della guerra di logoramento venne invocata per giustificare la tattica del massacro: "Abbiamo più uomini che il nemico, quindi prima uccidiamo i soldati nemici, prima saremo i vincitori".

Il grottesco corteo continuò la sua marcia.

Triumphant expectations. The declaration of war is read out in Berlin, August 1914.
'Let your hearts beat for God,' exhorted the Kaiser, 'and your fists on the enemy!'
In a surge of patriotism, men leapt at the chance to die.

Esperanzas de victoria. Lectura de la declaración de guerra en Berlín, en agosto de
1914. "Que vuestros corazones latan por Dios –exortó el káiser– y que vuestros
puños golpeen al enemigo." En un arranque de patriotismo, muchos hombres no
dejaron pasar la oportunidad de morir por la patria.

Speranze di vittoria. La dichiarazione di guerra viene letta in pubblico a Berlino,
nell'agosto del 1914. "Che i vostri cuori battano per Dio", esorta il Kaiser, "e i vostri
pugni battano il nemico!". In un impeto di patriottismo, gli uomini colsero al volo
l'occasione di morire per la patria.

Cheering crowds greet Britain's declaration of war on Germany in Trafalgar Square, London, 4 August 1914. Within a month, 17 million men across Europe were engaged in fighting.

Una multitud entusiasta celebra la declaración de guerra a Alemania en Trafalgar Square, Londres, el 4 de agosto de 1914. Un mes después, 17 millones de hombres en toda Europa eran reclutados.

Una folla entusiasta saluta la dichiarazione di guerra della Gran Bretagna alla Germania a Trafalgar Square (Londra), il 4 agosto 1914. In un mese, 17 milioni di europei furono coinvolti nei combattimenti.

Recruiting posters in Fleet Street, London, 1915. The message at the top reads: 'If you are a whiteman prove your colour and courage now'.

Carteles de reclutamiento en Fleet Street, Londres, 1915. El mensaje de más arriba reza: "Si eres un hombre blanco, ha llegado el momento de demostrar tu color y tu valentía".

Annunci di reclutamento a Fleet Street, Londra, 1915. L'annuncio in alto a destra recita: "Se sei bianco, adesso è il momento di dimostrare il tuo colore e il tuo coraggio".

Would-be soldiers take the King's Shilling and the oath of allegiance at a recruiting office in Shepherd's Bush, London, December 1914. They came in all ages and from all classes.

Tras recibir un chelín por alistarse, estos futuros soldados prestan juramento de fidelidad en una oficina de reclutamiento de Shepherd's Bush, Londres, en diciembre de 1914. Eran hombres de todas las edades y clases sociales.

I futuri soldati ricevono lo scellino del re in cambio del loro arruolamento e giurano fedeltà in un ufficio di reclutamento di Shepherd's Bush (Londra), nel dicembre del 1914. Le reclute, di tutte le età, provenivano da ogni classe sociale.

Newly-kitted-out recruits line up for inspection in Bermondsey, London, 1915. Men such as these formed the backbone of Kitchener's New Armies. Within months they would be in the front line.

Reclutas recién equipados en fila para una inspección en Bermondsey, Londres, 1915. Hombres como estos formaban la columna vertebral de los Nuevos Ejércitos de Kitchener. Unos meses después lucharían en el frente.

Reclute vestite di nuovo in fila per un'ispezione a Bermondsey (Londra) nel 1915. Questi uomini costituiscono la spina dorsale delle New Armies di Kitchener. Tra qualche mese saranno al fronte.

Two recruits receive their medical examination at Marylebone Grammar School, London, 1914. They were almost certainly among the first, for the school would have been requisitioned by the military for the summer holidays only.

Dos reclutas pasan un examen médico en la Marylebone Grammar School, Londres, en 1914. Seguramente eran de los primeros en ir a filas, ya que es probable que el ejército no pudiera requisar una escuela más que durante las vacaciones de verano.

Due reclute vengono sottoposte a un controllo medico nel liceo di Marylebone (Londra) nel 1914. Quasi sicuramente sono tra i primi coscritti, in quanto l'esercito non avrebbe potuto occupare la scuola dopo le vacanze estive.

Watched by anxious crowds, German troops march through the Place Rogier, Brussels, 20 August 1914. It had taken just over two weeks to reach the Belgian capital. The photograph was published in English and French newspapers.

Bajo la mirada ansiosa de la multitud, las tropas alemanas desfilan por la plaza Rogier de Bruselas, el 20 de agosto de 1914. Solo habían necesitado dos semanas para llegar a la capital belga. La fotografía se publicó en periódicos ingleses y franceses.

Sotto lo sguardo di una folla ansiosa, le truppe tedesche sfilano su place Rogier a Bruxelles, il 20 agosto 1914. In solo due settimane avevano raggiunto la capitale belga. Questa fotografia comparve sui giornali inglesi e francesi.

French reservists set out for army headquarters at the beginning of the First World War, August 1914. In 1913 the French Government had increased the period of compulsory military service to three years.

Reservistas franceses dirigiéndose a los cuarteles generales del ejército a comienzos de la Primera Guerra Mundial, en agosto de 1914. En 1913, el Gobierno francés había alargado la duración del servicio militar obligatorio a tres años.

Riservisti francesi in marcia verso i quartieri generali dell'esercito all'inizio della Prima guerra mondiale, nell'agosto 1914. Nel 1913, il governo francese aveva prolungato la durata del servizio militare di leva a tre anni.

'Goodbye, goodbye… wipe that tear, baby dear, from your eye…' – a British
soldier bids farewell to a loved one at Victoria Station, London, December 1914.
It was a scene that became tragically commonplace.

"Adiós, adiós… enjuga esa lágrima, que te cae por la mejilla, cariño." Un soldado
británico se despide de su amada en la estación de Victoria, Londres, en diciembre
de 1914. Por desgracia, la escena pasaría a ser demasiado habitual.

"Addio, addio… E basta lacrime, tesoro mio…" Un soldato britannico dice addio
alla sua fidanzata alla stazione Vittoria (Londra), dicembre 1914. Una scena che
divenne tristemente banale.

Families meet,
place flowers on
the helmets of their
heroes, and part,
as young German
soldiers leave for
the Front, 1914.

Las familias se
congregan y ponen
flores en los cascos
de sus héroes antes
de despedirse, como
en el caso de estos
jóvenes soldados
alemanes que parten
hacia el frente en
1914.

Le famiglie si
riuniscono e
decorano con fiori
i caschi dei loro eroi
in partenza. Questi
giovani tedeschi
stanno partendo
per il fronte (1914).

The United States entered the war in 1917 with orchestrated enthusiasm. Men and machines poured off the conveyor belt, as this picture of civilians being turned into 'rookies' suggests. American military propaganda was way ahead of that of other combatants.

Estados Unidos entró en la guerra en 1917 con un entusiasmo orquestado. Hombres y máquinas parecían salir de una cinta transportadora, tal como muestra esta fotografía de jóvenes transformados en "novatos". La propaganda militar americana superaba claramente a la de otros participantes.

Gli Stati Uniti entrano in guerra nel 1917 con un entusiasmo calcolato. Gli uomini e i fucili sembrano uscire da un rullo trasportatore, come suggerisce quest'immagine di civili trasformati in reclute. La propaganda militare americana è all'avanguardia rispetto a quella degli altri stati.

But this photograph of a bugle boy saying goodbye to his girl is almost certainly genuine, as is her grief.

Pero esta fotografía que recoge a un corneta despidiéndose de su amada parece verídica, como el dolor de la joven.

Ma questa fotografia di un trombettiere che dice addio alla sua fidanzata sembra autentica, come il dolore di quest'ultima.

Officers on a bridge address British
soldiers after the capture of the
St Quentin Canal, 1918. After three
and a half years of trench warfare,
armies were on the move once more.

Unos oficiales se dirigen a los
soldados británicos desde lo alto de
un puente tras la conquista del canal
de Saint-Quentin, en 1918. Después
de tres años y medio de guerra de
trincheras, los ejércitos se ponían
de nuevo en movimiento.

Degli ufficiali si rivolgono dall'alto
di un ponte a dei soldati britannici
dopo la conquista del canale di San
Quentin nel 1918. Dopo tre anni
e mezzo di trincee, gli eserciti
riprendono a muoversi.

In the heart of the heat, smoke and noise of battle – an American artillery unit in action on the Western Front at the St Mihiel Salient, a few miles south of Verdun, 27 September 1918.

En el fragor del combate. Una unidad de artillería estadounidense del frente occidental en acción en la punta de Saint-Mihiel, unos kilómetros al sur de Verdún, el 27 de septiembre de 1918.

Nel cuore del calore, del fumo e del rumore della battaglia: un'unità di artiglieria americana in azione sul fronte occidentale, nel bastione di Saint-Mihiel, qualche chilometro a sud di Verdun, il 27 settembre 1918.

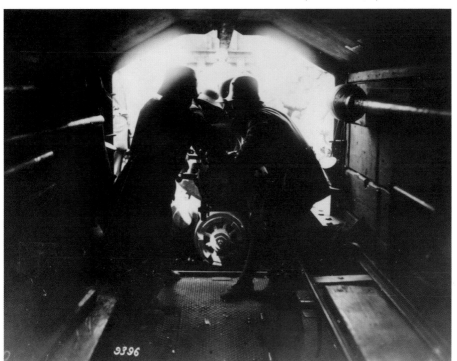

9396

German artillerymen load shells into a gun mounted on a railway train, 1914.
The original German strategy for the war was based on the Schlieffen Plan,
which depended on the use of the railways of north-west Europe.

Artilleros alemanes cargan municiones en un cañón montado en un tren,
en 1914. La estrategia de guerra original de Alemania se basaba en el
plan Schlieffen, que se centraba en el uso de los ferrocarriles del noroeste
de Europa.

Artiglieri tedeschi caricano con proiettili un cannone montato su un vagone,
1914. Il piano Schlieffen, che fu alla base di una nuova strategia di guerra per
i tedeschi, si basava sull'utilizzo delle ferrovie dell'Europa nord-occidentale.

The beauty and
terror of war.
A patrol freezes
as a flare lights up
no-man's land on
the Western Front.

La belleza y el
horror de la guerra.
Una patrulla se
queda inmóvil
cuando un destello
ilumina una franja
de tierra de nadie en
el frente occidental.

La bellezza e l'orrore
della guerra. Un
soldato di pattuglia
si immobilizza
mentre un razzo
illumina la terra di
nessuno del fronte
occidentale.

A tank looms over a shell crater on the Western Front, 1917. The new machine struck terror into the hearts of its occupants as well as the enemy. It was a shock weapon, but its ability to inflict damage was limited.

Un tanque surge imponente de un cráter en el frente occidental, en 1917. Esta nueva máquina sembraba el terror tanto entre sus ocupantes como entre los enemigos. Era un arma de choque pero su capacidad de destrucción era limitada.

Un carro armato emerge da un cratere sul fronte occidentale, 1917. Questa nuova macchina da guerra terrorizzava tanto il nemico quanto i suoi occupanti, ma la sua capacità di fare danni effettivi era limitata.

Big Bertha in action, 1917. The L14 Howitzer was the biggest gun in the world. It was manufactured by Krupp of Essen, had a range of 122 kilometres and bombarded Paris for more than a year and a half.

El gran Bertha en acción, en 1917. El Howitzer L14, fabricado por Krupp en Essen, era el cañón más grande del mundo. Tenía un alcance de 122 kilómetros y se utilizó para bombardear París durante más de un año y medio.

La grande Bertha in azione, 1917. L'Howitzer L14 era il cannone più grande del mondo. Fabbricato da Krupp a Essen, aveva una portata di 122 chilometri e fu utilizzato per bombardare Parigi per più di un anno e mezzo.

Possibly a genuine action shot of a German soldier hurling a grenade, but the figure on the far left suggests the photograph was staged.

Esta fotografía de un soldado alemán lanzando una granada parece auténtica, pero la figura que aparece en el extremo izquierdo de la imagen hace pensar que se trata de una puesta en escena.

Questa fotografia di un soldato tedesco che lancia una granata sembra spontanea, ma il personaggio all'estrema sinistra fa pensare che si tratti di una messa in scena.

(Above and opposite) Two scenes from the German advance at Villers-Bretonneaux, just to the east of Amiens, March 1918. (Above) A second wave of German troops passes a dead French infantryman in a shell hole.

(Arriba y página siguiente) Dos imágenes del avance alemán en Villers-Bretonneaux, al este de Amiens, en marzo de 1918. (Arriba) Una segunda oleada de tropas alemanas pasa junto a un soldado de infantería francés que yace en el cráter dejado por un obús.

(Sopra e accanto) Due scene che illustrano l'avanzata tedesca a Villers-Bretonneaux, a est di Amiens, marzo 1918. (Sopra) Una seconda ondata di soldati tedeschi passa davanti al cadavere di un fante francese ucciso dall'esplosione di una bomba.

Ludendorff's offensive almost broke the Allied line, but it managed to hold and turn the German attack. (Above) Some of the 3 million German troops on the Western Front at this time.

La ofensiva de Ludendorff casi rompió la línea aliada, pero esta resistió y contraatacó. (Arriba) Algunos de los tres millones de soldados alemanes desplegados en el frente occidental.

La linea degli Alleati fu quasi spezzata dall'offensiva di Ludendorff, ma riuscì a resistere e a contrattaccare. (Qui sopra) Alcuni dei tre milioni di soldati tedeschi del fronte occidentale.

Modern warfare. German soldiers (above) create a smokescreen during the First World War. (Opposite) British casualties, blinded by gas, await treatment near Béthune, 1918.

Técnicas de guerra modernas. Un grupo de soldados alemanes (arriba) crea una pantalla de humo durante la Primera Guerra Mundial. (Página siguiente) Heridos británicos, cegados por el gas, esperan a ser atendidos cerca de Béthune, en 1918.

Tecniche di guerra moderne. Soldati tedeschi (sopra) creano una cortina di fumo durante la Prima guerra mondiale. (Accanto) Feriti britannici, accecati dai gas, aspettano di essere curati vicino a Béthune, 1918.

Wounded Australian troops move back to a casualty clearing station on the Menin
Road, 1917. On the outbreak of war, the Australian Prime Minister announced:
'Our duty is quite clear – to gird up our loins and remember that we are Britons.'

Soldados australianos heridos se dirigen a un centro de atención sanitaria situado
en la carretera de Menin, en 1917. Cuando se declaró la guerra, el primer ministro
australiano afirmó: "Nuestro deber es muy sencillo: prepararnos para la lucha y
recordar que somos británicos".

Soldati australiani feriti ripiegano verso un'infermeria sulla strada per Menin,
1917. Allo scoppio della guerra, il Primo ministro australiano dichiarò: "Il nostro
dovere è molto semplice. Prendere il coraggio a due mani e non dimenticare che
siamo britannici".

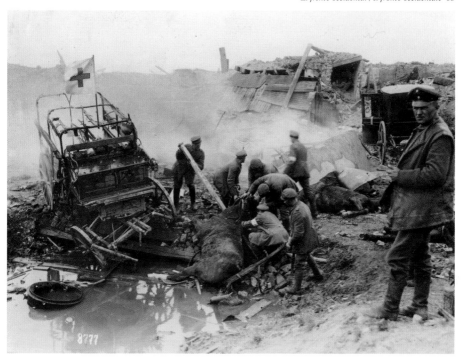

German soldiers search through the wreckage of a Red Cross truck, 1916. On both sides there were many men who refused to fight, but who died serving in non-combatant capacities.

Un grupo de soldados alemanes busca entre los restos de un camión de la Cruz Roja, en 1916. En ambos bandos hubo hombres que se negaron a luchar pero que murieron mientras realizaban operaciones civiles.

Soldati tedeschi frugano tra i resti di un camion della Croce Rossa, nel 1916. In entrambi i campi furono molti quelli che rifiutarono di combattere ma morirono servendo in operazioni civili.

The name Passchendaele passed into British military folklore as a living hell. Between July and November 1917 tens of thousands of men fought and died waist-deep in mud for possession of a few acres of derelict countryside.

En la jerga militar británica, el nombre de Passchendaele se convirtió en sinónimo de infierno. Entre julio y noviembre de 1917, decenas de miles de hombres lucharon y murieron hundidos en el barro para conquistar unas pocas hectáreas de campo abandonado.

Nel gergo militare britannico, il nome Passchendaele è diventato sinonimo di inferno in terra. Tra luglio e novembre del 1917, decine di migliaia di uomini lottarono e morirono col fango fino al petto, per conquistare qualche ettaro di una campagna saccheggiata.

(Opposite) A wounded soldier is carried by stretcher-bearers during the Battle of Passchendaele, 1 August 1917. (Above) Soldiers of the 16th Canadian Machine Gun Regiment in temporary defences at Passchendaele, 14 November 1917.

(Página anterior) Unos camilleros llevan a un soldado herido durante la batalla de Passchendaele, el 1 de agosto de 1917. (Arriba) Soldados del Decimosexto Regimiento de Fusileros Ametralladores Canadienses en los puestos de defensa temporales instalados en Passchendaele, el 14 de noviembre de 1917.

(Accanto) Un soldato ferito viene trasportato in barella durante la battaglia di Passchendaele, il 1º agosto 1917. (Sopra) Soldati del 16º reggimento canadese di fucilieri-mitragliatori alle loro postazioni di difesa temporanea a Passchendaele, 14 novembre 1917.

Canadian troops charge into action, 1916. The first Canadian contingent arrived in Europe in October 1914, more than 30,000 of them having been recruited and trained within two months of the outbreak of war.

Soldados canadienses listos para entrar en acción, en 1916. El primer contingente canadiense llegó a Europa en octubre de 1914. Más de 30.000 de sus integrantes habían sido reclutados y entrenados durante los dos meses posteriores al inicio de la guerra.

Soldati canadesi pronti a sparare nel 1916. Il primo contingente canadese arrivò in Europa nell'ottobre del 1914, e più di 30.000 di questi soldati erano stati arruolati e addestrati nei due mesi che seguirono l'inizio della guerra.

On the Western Front the slaughter continued unabated throughout the war. This picture of dead German troops was taken during the Battle of Cambrai at Flesquières, 23 November 1917.

En el frente occidental, la masacre no cesó durante toda la guerra. Esta imagen de soldados alemanes muertos fue tomada durante la batalla de Cambrai, en Flesquières, el 23 de noviembre de 1917.

Sul fronte occidentale, il massacro continuò senza tregua per tutta la guerra. Questa fotografia che mostra dei caduti tedeschi fu scattata durante la battaglia di Cambrai a Flesquières, il 23 novembre 1917.

British dead, killed while covering the retreat of their colleagues during the German Spring Offensive of 1918. When the fighting finally stopped in November 1918, neither side had gained any significant ground.

Soldados británicos abatidos cuando cubrían el repliegue de sus compañeros durante las ofensivas alemanas de la primavera de 1918. Cuando cesó la batalla, en noviembre de 1918, ninguno de los bandos había logrado un avance destacable.

Soldati britannici uccisi mentre coprono la ritirata dei loro compagni durante l'offensiva tedesca del primavera del 1918. A battaglia finita, nel novembre 1918, nessuna delle parti in campo aveva fatto progressi significativi.

Dark humour in wartime. French infantrymen use coffins as tables
while eating their dinner behind the lines, 1916. It was neither the
time nor the place for undue sensitivity.

Humor negro en tiempo de guerra. Soldados de la infantería francesa
de la retaguardia utilizan unos ataúdes como mesa para comer, en
1916. No era el momento ni el lugar para mostrarse escrupuloso.

Humor nero in tempi di guerra. Dietro le linee del fronte, i fanti
francesi mangiano su bare trasformate in tavoli, 1916. Non era
né il luogo né il momento di mostrare un'eccessiva sensibilità.

The night's kill. German troops display the rats killed in their trench the previous night, March 1916. The trench appears in good condition: it is unlikely that they were reduced to eating these rodents.

Matanza nocturna. Unos soldados muestran las ratas abatidas en la trinchera la noche anterior. La trinchera parece en buen estado, de manera que no se antoja probable que se vieran obligados a comerse esos roedores.

Conquista notturna. Soldati tedeschi presentano i ratti uccisi in trincea la notte precedente, marzo 1916. La trincea sembra in buono stato, pertanto è poco probabile che siano costretti a nutrirsi di questi roditori.

Learning his trade. Corporal Adolf Hitler (right) with two comrades in the early days of the First World War.

Aprendizaje. El cabo Adolf Hitler (derecha) con dos compañeros al comienzo de la Primera Guerra Mundial.

Addestramento. Il caporale Adolf Hitler (a destra) con due camerati all'inizio della Prima guerra mondiale.

Out of office. Winston Churchill (right), Colonel of the Royal Scots Fusiliers, at Armentières, 11 February 1916.

Descanso. Winston Churchill (derecha), coronel de los Royal Scots Fusiliers, en Armentières, el 11 de febrero de 1916.

Riposo. Winston Churchill (a destra), colonnello dei Royal Scots Fusiliers, a Armentières l'11 febbraio 1916.

3. The home front
El frente en casa
Il fronte a casa

A soldier on leave goes Christmas shopping with his family – a scene of 'wishful thinking'. Workers in war-related industries earned good money, but the average 'Tommy' was poorly paid.

Un soldado de permiso y su familia hacen las compras de Navidad –o por lo menos anhelan poder hacerlas–. Los trabajadores de la industria bélica estaban bien pagados, pero los simples soldados percibían un salario muy modesto.

Un soldato in licenza e la sua famiglia fanno gli acquisti di Natale – una scena che dimostra come si possa vivere di illusioni. Gli operai delle industrie belliche erano ben pagati, ma il soldato semplice riceveva un salario molto modesto.

3. The home front
El frente en casa
Il fronte a casa

Civilians gave flowers to departing soldiers and white feathers to those they regarded as cowards. They knitted 'comforts' for the troops and turned parks over to vegetables. They attacked the shops and businesses of enemy aliens and rushed for shelter during the intermittent air-raids.

The struggle was to maintain a semblance of 'business as usual'. Many saw it as their duty to keep theatres, dance-halls and picture palaces open; to dance and dine at fine restaurants. How else would men returning on leave from the Front have a good time and be reminded of what they were fighting for?

But the war bit savagely into the lives of everyone. Few families escaped the horror of losing a husband, a son, a brother or a father. The whole of Europe became accustomed to the living scars of war – to men who had lost their sight, their limbs, their senses.

Black marketeers 'throve like maggots in an apple'. By August 1916 there was no milk or cheese to be bought on the open market in Berlin, and butchers were offering crows, squirrels and woodpeckers for sale. The people kept on praying.

Los civiles regalaban flores a los soldados que partían al frente y plumas blancas a quienes consideraban unos cobardes. Tejían "talismanes" para los soldados y transformaban los parques en huertos. Atacaban los comercios y las empresas que pertenecían a extranjeros enemigos de la patria y corrían a los refugios cada vez que se producía un ataque aéreo.

Pese a las tristes circunstancias, había que esforzarse y hacer como si nada pasara. Muchas personas creían que era su deber mantener los teatros, las salas de bailes y los cines abiertos; o ir a bailar y a comer a buenos restaurantes. De lo contrario, ¿cómo podrían divertirse y recordar por qué luchaban los soldados que estuvieran de permiso?

Pero la guerra golpeó con fuerza en la vida de todos. Pocas familias escaparon al horror de perder un marido, un hijo, un hermano o un padre. Toda Europa tuvo que acostumbrarse a las cicatrices de la guerra, a hombres que perdían la vida, alguna extremidad o incluso la razón.

El mercado negro floreció. En agosto de 1916, ya no se podía comprar leche o queso en las tiendas de Berlín y los tenderos vendían cuervos, ardillas y pájaros carpinteros. Mientras, la gente seguía rezando.

I civili distribuivano fiori ai soldati che partivano per la guerra e piume bianche a quelli che consideravano codardi. Confezionavano "mascotte" per le truppe e trasformavano i parchi in orti. Attaccavano i negozi e le ditte appartenenti a paesi nemici e si riparavano nei rifugi durante gli attacchi aerei.

E, malgrado tutto, cercavano di mantenere una parvenza di normalità. Molti, infatti, pensavano che fosse loro dovere mantenere aperti i teatri, le sale da ballo e i cinema, andare a ballare e mangiare in ristoranti eccellenti. Altrimenti, come avrebbero fatto i soldati in licenza a passare momenti piacevoli e ricordare per cosa stavano combattendo?

Ma la guerra morse selvaggiamente la vita di ciascuno. Poche famiglie ebbero la fortuna di non perdere un marito, un figlio, un fratello o un padre. Tutta l'Europa dovette abituarsi alle ferite aperte del conflitto, a vedere uomini che avevano perso la vista, un arto o la ragione.

Chi vendeva al mercato nero faceva affari d'oro: nell'agosto del 1916 non era più possibile acquistare latte o formaggio nei negozi di Berlino e i macellai vendevano corvi, scoiattoli e picchi. La gente continuava a pregare.

The queue for the air-raid shelter, Hither Green, London, October 1917. Bombing raids by Zeppelins were becoming more frequent by now.

Cola para entrar en un refugio antiaéreo en Hither Green, Londres, en octubre de 1917. Por aquel entonces, cada vez eran más frecuentes los bombardeos de los zepelines.

Coda per rifugiarsi in un rifugio antiaereo a Hither Green (Londra), ottobre 1917. In quest'epoca, i bombardamenti effettuati dagli Zeppelin si stavano intensificando.

A woman munitions worker at Vickers, 1915. Most women preferred such work to domestic service. 'It was much more comfortable, it was more money... I was on two or three pounds a week... with all the girls it was like a jolly party' – Lil Truphet.

Obrera de una fábrica de municiones de Vickers, en 1915. La mayoría de las mujeres preferían este trabajo a las tareas del hogar. "Era mucho más cómodo, daba más dinero... Ganaba dos o tres libras por semana... y siempre nos divertíamos con las demás chicas" (Lil Truphet).

Operaia in una fabbrica di munizioni a Vickers, 1915. La maggioranza delle donne preferivano questo tipo di lavoro alle faccende domestiche. "Era meno faticoso e meglio pagato... Io prendevo due o tre sterline a settimana... e con le altre ragazze ci si divertiva un sacco" (Lil Truphet).

A recruiting march through London by members of the Women's Auxiliary Army Corps, 1915. For young women, the armed forces offered a more exciting life and greater freedom than they would have enjoyed at home.

Marcha par la movilización organizada por miembros de los Cuerpos del Ejército Auxiliar de Mujeres, en 1915. Para las mujeres jóvenes, las fuerzas armadas ofrecían una vida más emocionante y más libertad de la que hubieran tenido en sus casas.

Marcia per il reclutamento organizzata dalle donne del Women's Auxiliary Army Corps attraverso Londra, 1915. Per le giovani, l'esercito offriva una vita più eccitante e una libertà molto maggiore rispetto a restare a casa.

Public disgrace. A conscientious objector is made to sit in specially built stocks, 1916. Painted on the seat is the slogan 'This is for traitors'. Conscription had come to Britain for the first time.

Escarnio público. Un objetor de conciencia es obligado a sentarse en una especie de picota, en 1916. En el respaldo reza la leyenda: "Para los traidores". Por primera vez, el servicio militar era obligatorio en Gran Bretaña.

Disgrazia pubblica. Un obiettore di coscienza viene fatto sedere su una speciale gogna, 1916. Lo slogan sullo schienale dice "Per i traditori". Per la prima volta, il servizio militare è obbligatorio in Gran Bretagna.

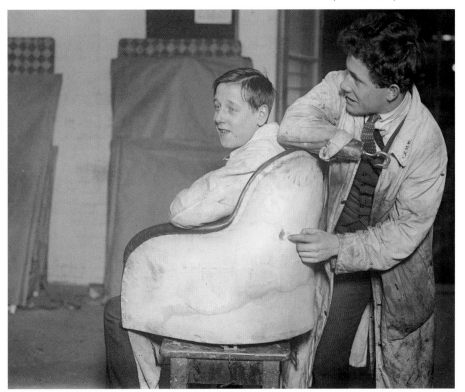

Private disability. Two limbless ex-servicemen examine the seat from a German Gotha bomber at Lord Roberts' Memorial Workshop in the Brompton Road, London, December 1917.

Desgracia privada. Dos ex soldados mutilados examinan el asiento de un bombardero alemán Gotha expuesto en el Lord Robert's Memorial Workshop en Brompton Road, Londres, en diciembre de 1917.

Disgrazia personale. Due ex-soldati mutilati esaminano il sedile di un bombardiere tedesco Gotha esposto al Lord Robert's Memorial Workshop di Brompton Road (Londra), nel dicembre del 1917.

Lady Diana Manners (in nurse's uniform) collects funds for 'Our Day', 19 October 1916. The British army had just suffered its worst ever losses in battle. The aim of the collection was to provide food and tobacco for the survivors.

Lady Diana Manners (con uniforme de enfermera) recauda fondos para "Our Day", el 19 de octubre de 1916. El ejército británico acababa de sufrir las mayores pérdidas de su historia en el campo de batalla. El objetivo de la recaudación era ofrecer comida y tabaco a los supervivientes.

Lady Diana Manners (con l'uniforme da infermiera) raccoglie fondi per la giornata "Our Day", il 19 ottobre 1916. L'esercito britannico aveva appena registrato le perdite più gravi dall'inizio della guerra. I fondi raccolti sarebbero serviti per fornire cibo e tabacco ai reduci.

Soldiers and sailors attend the mass funeral of victims of the *Lusitania* disaster, May 1915.
The sinking of the Cunard liner by German torpedoes, with the loss of 1,198 lives, provided
a propaganda coup for the British Government.

Soldados y marineros asisten a los funerales colectivos de las víctimas del desastre del *Lusitania*,
en mayo de 1915. El hundimiento del buque de la compañía Cunard por los torpedos alemanes,
que se saldó con 1.198 muertes, fue un gran golpe de propaganda para el Gobierno británico.

Soldati e marinai partecipano al funerale collettivo delle vittime del disastro del *Lusitania*, maggio
1915. Il naufragio del piroscafo della Cunard, affondato dai tedeschi e nel cui naufragio
morirono 1198 persone, fu un'occasione di propaganda per il governo britannico.

The fruits of Empire. During a potato shortage, a market trader offers pineapples as an alternative, 1 February 1917. How many takers he found at ninepence (4p) each, we do not know.

Los frutos del Imperio. A falta de patatas, un comerciante ofrece piñas como alternativa, el 1 de febrero de 1917. Lo que no sabemos es cuántos compradores conseguiría a nueve peniques la unidad.

I frutti dell'Impero. In mancanza di patate, un fruttivendolo vende ananas, 1° febbraio 1917. Resta da sapere quanti ne venderà, a un ninepence (4p) al pezzo.

The seeds of hope. London and South West railwaymen head for railway waste ground to plant their sacks of seed potatoes, April 1917. Golf courses and even cricket fields became vegetable gardens during the war.

Semillas de esperanza. Ferroviarios de Londres y del suroeste se dirigen a los grandes terrenos de las líneas ferroviarias para plantar patatas, en abril de 1917. Los campos de golf y de *cricket* también se transformaron en huertos improvisados durante la guerra.

I semi della speranza. Ferrovieri di Londra e del Sud-Ovest si dirigono verso i terreni abbandonati delle ferrovie per piantarvi delle patate, aprile 1917. I campi da golf e persino quelli da cricket furono trasformati in orti durante la guerra.

Voluntary workers at the British War Library pack parcels of books to be despatched to troops on active service, 24 August 1916. Reading helped combat the boredom of trench warfare.

Trabajadores voluntarios de la Biblioteca Militar Británica empaquetan libros para enviarlos a las tropas, el 24 de agosto de 1916. La lectura ayudaba a combatir el aburrimiento de la guerra de trincheras.

Volontari della Biblioteca militare britannica preparano pacchetti di libri da inviare alle truppe in servizio, 24 agosto 1916. Leggere era un modo per combattere la noia della guerra di trincea.

Assembling parcels of food and other comforts for British prisoners of war in Germany, 1916. 'Other comforts' might include clothing, games, books and magazines, and – on at least one occasion – cricket balls.

Preparación de paquetes de comida y otras comodidades para los prisioneros de guerra británicos en Alemania, 1916. "Otras comodidades" significaba, por ejemplo, ropa, juegos, libros, revistas e incluso, al menos en una ocasión, pelotas de *cricket*.

Confezione di pacchetti di cibo e altri generi per i prigionieri britannici detenuti in Germania, 1916. Gli altri generi potevano comprendere abiti, giocattoli, libri, riviste e persino palle da cricket.

Wounded soldiers, wearing a new type of crutch fitted to the belt, attempt to topple a 'Kokonut Kaiser' at a fair in Sidcup, Kent, 1 September 1917. Much wry humour and hatred was directed towards the German Emperor during the war.

Soldados heridos, con un nuevo tipo de muleta fijada al cinturón, tratan de derribar una imagen del káiser en una feria celebrada en Sidcup, Kent, el 1 de septiembre de 1917. Durante la guerra, el emperador alemán fue objeto de numerosas burlas que, en no pocas ocasiones, estaban cargadas de odio.

Dei soldati feriti, con un nuovo tipo di stampelle fissate alla cintura, tentano di rovesciare l'imperatore al gioco 'Kokonut Kaiser' dei baracconi di Sidcup (Kent), 1° settembre 1917. Durante la guerra, il Kaiser fu frequentemente oggetto di scherno e astio.

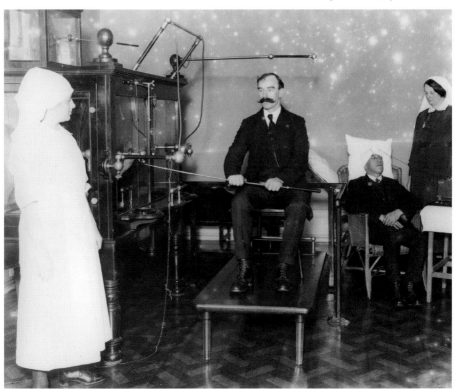

Nurses at a hospital in Britain superintend the use of experimental new apparatus for soldiers suffering from shell-shock, 1917. It took a long time for the medical profession to accept that such a condition was genuine.

Enfermeras de un hospital británico supervisan la utilización de dispositivos experimentales destinados a los soldados traumatizados por la explosión de los obuses, en 1917. La profesión médica tardó mucho tiempo en aceptar que dicha dolencia era real.

Infermiere di un ospitale britannico sorvegliano l'utilizzo di apparecchi sperimentali destinati ai soldati in stato di choc, 1917. I medici riconobbero che tale condizione era autentica solo dopo molto tempo.

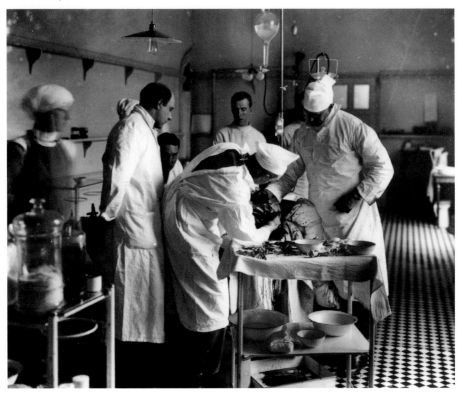

An amputation in progress at the Duchess of Westminster Military
Hospital, 1915. The route from battlefield to well-equipped hospital
for such an operation was often a slow and painful one.

Amputación en curso en el hospital militar Duchess of Westminster,
en 1915. El trayecto del campo de batalla a un hospital bien equipado
para este tipo de operación era, por lo general, largo y doloroso.

Amputazione in corso presso l'ospedale militare Duchess of Westminster,
1915. Il tragitto dal campo di battaglia a un ospedale attrezzato per
questo tipo di operazioni era spesso lungo e doloroso.

Soldiers attend a charity concert at the Savoy Hotel, London, March 1916. Privately, many hoped for a 'Blighty' wound – one serious enough for them to be sent home, but not permanently disabling. Few were so lucky.

Soldados en un concierto benéfico en el Hotel Savoy de Londres, en marzo de 1916. En su fuero interno, muchos esperaban sufrir una herida lo bastante grave como para justificar su regreso a casa, pero no lo suficiente como para quedar incapacitados el resto de sus vidas. Fueron pocos los que tuvieron esa suerte.

Soldati a un concerto di beneficenza al Savoy Hotel di Londra nel marzo del 1916. Intimamente, molti speravano di rimanere feriti abbastanza gravemente da essere rimpatriati ma senza rimanere invalidi a vita. Pochi ebbero questa fortuna.

Playing at soldiers. The Lord Mayor of London (third from left) and his officials
visit the mock-up of a trench at an Active Services Exhibition in Knightsbridge,
London, March 1916.

Interpretando a soldados. El alcalde de Londres (tercero por la izquierda) y
sus funcionarios visitan la reconstrucción de una trinchera en el marco de una
exposición en los campos de honor en Knightsbridge, Londres, en marzo de 1916.

Giocare ai soldati. Il sindaco di Londra (il terzo da sinistra) e i suoi assistenti
visitano la ricostruzione di una trincea realizzata per una mostra sulle forze
attive a Knightsbrigdge (Londra), marzo 1916.

Soldiers at play. American troops enjoy donkey rides on the sands at Southport, Lancashire, 6 June 1918. From June 1917 they arrived in Europe at the rate of 50,000 every month.

Soldados jugando. Unos militares estadounidenses se divierten montando en burro en la playa de Southport, Lancashire, el 6 de junio de 1918. Desde junio de 1917 llegaron a Europa a un ritmo de 50.000 al mes.

Soldati che giocano. Dei militari americani si divertono a cavalcare degli asini sulla spiaggia di Southport (Lancashire), 6 giugno 1918. Dal giugno del 1917, sbarcarono in Europa al ritmo di 50.000 al mese.

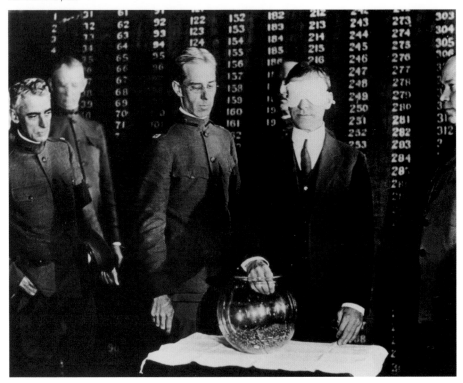

Under the terms of the Selective Draft Act of May 1917 every American male
between 21 and 30 years old had to register for national service. Each was given
a number. Here the numbers of those to be drafted are picked by lottery.

Según la ley de reclutamiento obligatorio (Selective Draft Act) de mayo de 1917,
todos los varones estadounidenses de entre 21 y 30 años debían alistarse para el
servicio militar y a cada uno se le asignaba un número. La imagen recoge la elección
al azar de los números de quienes serían movilizados.

La legge sulla coscrizione selettiva del maggio del 1917 obbligava tutti gli americani
tra i 21 e i 30 anni a registrarsi per il servizio militare. Ognuno riceveva un numero e,
come mostra questa foto, si estraeva a sorte chi doveva partire.

Americans are encouraged to sign a Declaration of Patriotism following the United States' decision to enter the war, April 1917.

Campaña para animar a los estadounidenses a firmar una "Declaración de patriotismo" tras la decisión de Estados Unidos de entrar en guerra, en abril de 1917.

Gli americani sono incoraggiati a firmare una "Dichiarazione di patriottismo" dopo la decisione degli Stati Uniti di entrare in guerra, nell'aprile del 1917.

Although it had been proved that the cavalry had little part to play in modern warfare, a squadron of American cavalrymen show their horsemanship, 1917. The days of Teddy Roosevelt's Rough Riders were over.

Aunque había quedado demostrado que la caballería ya no tenía cabida en las guerras modernas, un escuadrón de soldados estadounidenses muestra sus habilidades con los caballos, en 1917. La época de los Rough Riders de Teddy Roosevelt ya había pasado a la historia.

Benché, come tutti sanno, la cavalleria non abbia più molta importanza nelle guerre moderne, questa squadra americana dimostra la sua maestria nell'arte equestre, 1917. I tempi dei Rough Riders di Teddy Roosevelt sono ormai passati.

A group of black GIs, 1918. There were many whites in the United States who frowned upon the idea of arming African-Americans, and many blacks who disliked the idea of fighting the white man's war. In the end, more than 400,000 blacks enlisted.

Un grupo de soldados estadounidenses negros, en 1918. En Estados Unidos, muchos blancos se oponían a la idea de armar a los afroamericanos y, por su parte, a muchos negros no les hacía ninguna gracia luchar en una guerra de hombres blancos. Al final, se enrolaron más de 400.000 reclutas negros.

Gruppo di G.I. neri, 1918. Negli Stati Uniti molti furono i bianchi che si opposero all'arruolamento di neri. Almeno altrettanti neri erano contrari a combattere una guerra di bianchi. Alla fine, furono più di 400.000 i neri che si arruolarono.

Cossack soldiers stroll through the streets of London, 1916. One of the early myths of the war was that an army of Cossacks had passed through England one night on their way to the Western Front 'with snow on their boots'.

Soldados cosacos en las calles de Londres, en 1916. Uno de los primeros mitos de la guerra fue que una noche un ejército de cosacos "con nieve en las botas" había cruzado Londres en dirección al frente occidental.

Cosacchi passeggiano per le strade di Londra, nel 1916. Secondo uno dei primi miti della guerra, una notte un esercito di cosacchi aveva attraversato l'Inghilterra con "la neve sugli stivali" per raggiungere il fronte occidentale.

A crowd gathers outside a small shop in the East End of London, June 1915. The owners have painted 'We are Russians' on the shop front, to protect themselves from anti-German vandalism.

Una multitud se congrega frente a una pequeña tienda del East End de Londres, en junio de 1915. Para protegerse del vandalismo antialemán, los propietarios del comercio escribieron en su exterior "Somos rusos".

Una folla si riunisce davanti a un negozietto dell'East End (Londra), giugno 1915. I proprietari hanno scritto "Siamo russi" sull'ingresso per proteggersi da atti di vandalismo anti-tedesco.

4. The wider war
La guerra en el mundo
La guerra nel mondo

Russian prisoners of war are marched away after their defeat at the Masurian Lakes in East Prussia, May 1915. From the very beginning of the war, the Russian army was ill-clad and ill-equipped.

Retirada de prisioneros de guerra rusos tras su derrota en los lagos de Mazuria, en Prusia oriental, en mayo de 1915. Desde el principio de la guerra, el ejército ruso estuvo mal ataviado y mal equipado.

Prigionieri russi dopo la sconfitta presso i laghi Masuri nella Prussia orientale. Sin dall'inizio della guerra l'esercito russo fu mal vestito e mal equipaggiato.

4. The wider war
La guerra en el mundo
La guerra nel mondo

More than 10 million men were killed in the First World War. Another 21 million were wounded. Although the Western Front was the most concentrated area of slaughter, losses on the Eastern Front were as great. Men died as far south as the Falkland Islands, as far north as the Arctic Circle. They died off the eastern seaboard of the United States and in the heat and dust of Mesopotamia. Gunboats engaged each other in Pacific atolls and in the creeks of Africa. It was the worst global catastrophe since the Black Death in the 1340s.

Men came from all over to the fields of carnage: Australians and New Zealanders died at Gallipoli; Canadians heroically stormed Vimy Ridge. Turkish soldiers fought a *jihad*, a Muslim holy war, against the infidels in Syria, bombarding thousands of Indian troops in the British garrison at Kut. The army which General Allenby led into Jerusalem included men from Singapore, Hong Kong and the West Indies.

In Europe few countries escaped active involvement. Men died in Hungary, Serbia, Italy, Romania, Bulgaria, Poland, Russia and a dozen other principalities. The contagion of madness was complete. War touched and contaminated every continent in the world.

Más de 10 millones de hombres murieron en la Primera Guerra Mundial y otros 21 millones resultaron heridos. Aunque el frente occidental fue la zona en que se concentraron las mayores masacres, las pérdidas en el frente oriental fueron asimismo importantes. Fallecieron hombres en todas partes: desde las islas Falkland, en el sur del globo, hasta el círculo ártico. Otros perdieron la vida en la costa este de Estados Unidos y en el calor y el polvo de Mesopotamia. Hubo combates entre lanchas cañoneras en los atolones del Pacífico y en los ríos africanos. Fue la mayor catástrofe mundial desde la peste negra de la década de 1340.

Hombres llegados de todas partes se enfrentaron en el campo de batalla: australianos y neozelandeses murieron en Gallipoli; canadienses conquistaron heróicamente la cresta de Vimy. Soldados turcos llevaron a cabo una *jihad* –guerra santa musulmana– contra los infieles en Siria, bombardeando a miles de soldados indios de la guarnición británica de Kut. El ejército con el que entró en Jerusalén el general Allenby estaba formado por hombres de Singapur, Hong Kong y las Antillas.

En Europa, fueron pocos los países que no participaron activamente. Hubo bajas en Hungría, Serbia, Italia, Rumanía, Bulgaria, Polonia, Rusia y otra docena de principados. La locura fue general. La guerra tocó y contaminó todos los continentes del mundo.

La Prima guerra mondiale fece più di 10 milioni di morti e 21 milioni di feriti. Benché i massacri abbiano avuto luogo principalmente sul fronte occidentale, le perdite umane sul fronte orientale furono altrettanto numerose. I soldati morivano nel Sud del mondo, nelle isole Falkland e nel circolo polare artico. Altri persero la vita sulle coste orientali degli Stati Uniti e nella calda e polverosa Mesopotamia. Le cannoniere si scontrarono negli atolli del Pacifico e nelle insenature africane. Fu la peggior catastrofe mondiale dopo la Peste Nera del 1340.

Uomini provenienti da ogni dove si ritrovarono sui campi di battaglia: soldati australiani e neozelandesi morirono a Gallipoli, i canadesi conquistarono eroicamente Vimy Ridge. I soldati turchi condussero una guerra santa islamica contro gli infedeli della Siria bombardando migliaia di soldati indiani della guarnigione britannica a Kut. L'esercito che entrò a Gerusalemme guidato dal generale Allenby era composto, tra gli altri, da soldati di Singapore, di Hong-Kong e delle Antille.

In Europa furono pochi i paesi non coinvolti direttamente nel conflitto. Vi furono morti in Ungheria, Serbia, Italia, Romania, Bulgaria, Polonia, Russia e un'altra dozzina di paesi. Il mondo fu colpito da un'epidemia di follia. La guerra toccò tutti i continenti del mondo.

Russian gunners
work their light field
guns in direct line-
of-sight formation
on the Eastern
Front, 1914.

Artilleros rusos
maniobran sus
cañones ligeros
para colocarlos en
posición en el frente
oriental, en 1914.

Artiglieri russi
posizionano
leggeri cannoni da
campo sul fronte
orientale, 1914.

A Russian regimental band accompanies troops to the Front, 23 June 1915. Most
regiments had their own band and their own priest. Which of the two did more
for morale is unknown.

La banda de un regimiento ruso acompaña a los soldados al frente, el 23 de junio
de 1915. La mayoría de los regimientos tenían su propia banda y su propio sacerdote.
Lo que no se sabe es cuál de los dos era capaz de levantar más la moral.

La fanfara di un reggimento russo accompagna i soldati al fronte, 23 giugno 1915.
La maggior parte dei reggimenti disponeva di una fanfara e un prete. Non ci si chieda
quale dei due fosse più utile per il morale.

A unit of Cossack infantry on the march, 1915. Many Russian regiments traditionally had at least one boy-soldier as a mascot, but all-out modern warfare was no place for mascots.

Unidad de infantería cosaca en marcha, en 1915. Muchos regimientos rusos llevaban tradicionalmente un niño soldado como mascota, pero en la guerra total moderna no había lugar para éstos.

Unità della fanteria cosacca in marcia, 1915. Tradizionalmente, i reggimenti russi avevano almeno un bambino-soldato come mascotte. La guerra totale moderna non prevede più questa figura.

German troops block railway lines on the Eastern Front, 1917. At this stage of the war they were looking for bands of pillaging irregular soldiers.

Un grupo de soldados alemanes bloquea las vías férreas en el frente oriental, en 1917. En este momento de la guerra, buscaban bandas de soldados saqueadores.

Soldati tedeschi bloccano la ferrovia sul fronte orientale, 1917. In questa fase della guerra, i soldati commettevano occasionalmente atti di saccheggio.

In the last days of the war in the east, a Russian soldier equipped with full anti-gas apparatus advances across no-man's land, 1917. The Tsar had already abdicated: the end was near for his armies.

Unos días antes de que finalizara la guerra en el este, un soldado equipado con un dispositivo anti gas completo avanza por tierra de nadie, en 1917. El zar ya había abdicado y se avecinaba el final de la guerra para sus ejércitos.

A qualche giorno dalla fine della guerra sul fronte orientale, un soldato russo munito di maschera a gas si avventura nella "terra di nessuno", 1917. Lo zar aveva già abdicato: la fine è prossima per il suo esercito.

German soldiers enter the looted and burning town of Szawle, 1918. The war was officially over in the east, but years were to pass before law and order returned to the region.

Los soldados alemanes entran en la ciudad de Szawle, pasto del pillaje y de las llamas, en 1918. La guerra ya había acabado oficialmente en el este, pero pasarían años antes de que la ley y el orden volvieran a instaurarse en la región.

Soldati tedeschi entrano nella città di Szawle saccheggiata e incendiata, 1918. Ufficialmente, la guerra a est è finita, ma ci vorranno anni prima che la legge e la stabilità tornino a regnare in questa regione.

Russian troops
throw down their
guns and surrender,
1917. To the front
was the German
army, to the rear
a divided country.
They had little
alternative.

Un grupo de
soldados rusos tira
sus armas y se rinde,
en 1917. Delante
tenían al ejército
alemán y detrás,
un país dividido.
No les quedaban
muchas alternativas.

Soldati russi
gettano le armi
e si arrendono,
1917. Davanti
a loro, l'esercito
tedesco e dietro,
un paese diviso.
Non avevano molte
alternative.

In the wake of the Russian Revolution, Finnish Communists and Social Democrats rose against their right-wing government in January 1918. An all-out civil war followed, in which whole towns were destroyed.

En los albores de la revolución rusa, los comunistas y los socialdemócratas finlandeses se sublevaron contra su Gobierno conservador en enero de 1918. A continuación se produjo una guerra civil total que causó la destrucción de ciudades enteras.

Sull'onda della rivoluzione russa, i comunisti e i socialdemocratici finlandesi si sollevarono contro il loro governo conservatore nel gennaio del 1918. Il risultato fu una vera e propria guerra civile, durante la quale vennero distrutte città intere.

'White' counter-revolutionary prisoners of the Red Guard are marched down the street. The rising was eventually crushed by White Army troops, and some 23,000 'Reds' were killed.

Contrarrevolucionarios "blancos", prisioneros de la Guardia Roja, son llevados por la calle. El levantamiento acabó siendo aplastado por los soldados del ejército blanco y murieron cerca de 23.000 "rojos".

Contro-rivoluzionari 'bianchi' prigionieri della Guardia Rossa vengono trasportati a piedi. Alla fine, la rivolta fu sedata dall'esercito bianco e 23.000 "rossi" furono uccisi.

A quiet day at Anzac Cove on
the Gallipoli Peninsula, 1915.
The campaign was one of the
most ill-conceived of the war.

Día de descanso en Anzac Cove,
en la península de Gallipoli, en 1915.
Esta campaña fue una de las peor
organizadas de la guerra.

Una giornata tranquilla a Anzac
Cove, nella penisola di Gallipoli,
1915. Questa campagna fu una delle
peggio organizzate di tutta la guerra.

Ernest Brooks's
photograph of a
60-pounder
heavy field gun
bombarding Turkish
positions at Helles
Bay, Gallipoli
(Gelibolu), 1915.

Fotografía de Ernest
Brooks de un cañón
de 60 libras
bombardeando
posiciones turcas en
la bahía de Helles,
Gallipoli, en 1915.

Cannone di 60
libbre inglesi
bombarda posizioni
turche nella baia di
Helles a Gallipoli.
Fotografia di Ernest
Brooks, 1915.

Fires destroy a section of the city of Constantinople, 1916. Britain confidently
expected to capture the city but never did. It was occupied by British troops,
however, after the war.

El fuego destruye una parte de Constantinopla, en 1916. Los británicos
confiaban en conquistar la ciudad pero nunca lo lograron. Sin embargo,
la localidad fue ocupada por los soldados británicos después de la guerra.

Incendi distruggono una parte della città di Costantinopoli, 1916. La Gran
Bretagna, certa di potersi impossessare della città, in realtà non vi riuscì mai.
La città fu invece occupata dai soldati britannici dopo la guerra.

Turkish troops undergoing training. Despite occasional debacles and some appalling leadership, the fighting qualities of the Turkish armies were much respected by Allied soldiers.

Soldados turcos en pleno entrenamiento. A pesar de algunas derrotas sonadas y varios dirigentes desastrosos, los ejércitos turcos eran muy respetados por los soldados aliados por sus aptitudes para el combate.

Soldati turchi durante l'addestramento. Malgrado alcune sconfitte e qualche comandante disastroso, le qualità militari dell'esercito turco erano molto rispettate dai soldati alleati.

(Opposite) Perhaps the most romantic figure of the war – T E Lawrence, in Arab dress, 1918. (Above) Lawrence of Arabia with his guerrilla troops in the desert, July 1917.

(Página anterior) Probablemente, el personaje más romántico de la guerra: T. E. Lawrence, vestido de árabe, en 1918. (Arriba) Lawrence de Arabia con sus guerrilleros en el desierto, en julio de 1917.

(Accanto) T. E. Lawrence, probabilmente il personaggio più romantico della guerra, vestito con abiti arabi, 1918. (Sopra) Lawrence d'Arabia e il suo esercito di guerriglieri nel deserto, luglio 1917.

A British officer poses with his Japanese counterpart beside a heavily camouflaged gun, at Tsingtao (now Qingdao), China, on the Yellow Sea, 1914. Britain maintained a military presence in the Far East.

Un oficial británico posa con sus homólogos japoneses junto a un cañón camuflado en Tsingtao (actual Quingdao), China, en el mar Amarillo, en 1914. Gran Bretaña mantuvo su presencia militar en Extremo Oriente.

Un ufficiale britannico posa con i suoi omologhi giapponesi davanti a un cannone ben camuffato, a Tsingtao (oggi Qingdao) in Cina, sulle rive del mar Giallo, 1914. La Gran Bretagna mantenne una presenza militare in Estremo Oriente.

A wounded orderly from the Royal Army Medical Corps is carried on a Chinese wheelbarrow, Tsingtao, China, 1914. He was a victim of one of the last colonial actions in this part of the world.

Un camillero herido del cuerpo médico del Royal Army es evacuado en una carretilla china, Tsingtao, China, en 1914. Fue víctima de una de las últimas acciones coloniales que se produjeron en esta parte del mundo.

Un infermiere ferito appartenente al corpo medico della Royal Army viene portato via su un aratro cinese a Tsingtao in Cina, 1914. Fu vittima di una delle ultime azioni coloniali intraprese in questa parte del mondo.

Serbian troops test the accuracy of captured Austrian rifles, Belgrade, 1915. The spark that had set the world ablaze at Sarajevo a year earlier was steadily destroying the Austro-Hungarian Empire.

Un grupo de soldados serbios comprueba la precisión de unos fusiles austriacos de los que se habían incautado, Belgrado, en 1915. La chispa que había prendido fuego al mundo en Sarajevo un año antes estaba destruyendo el imperio austrohúngaro.

Dei soldati serbi verificano la precisione dei fucili austriaci requisiti, Belgrado, 1915. La scintilla che aveva fatto esplodere il mondo a Sarajevo un anno prima distrusse progressivamente l'Impero austro-ungarico.

A Serbian soldier is given a shave in the trenches. This was one of several pictures from a series called 'Scenes with our Serbian Allies', published in Britain. The Serbs were regarded as gallant fighters and steadfast allies.

Sesión de afeitado para un soldado serbio en las trincheras. Esta fotografía formaba parte de una serie titulada: "La vida con nuestros aliados serbios", publicada en Gran Bretaña. A los serbios se les consideraba aguerridos luchadores y fieles aliados.

Un soldato serbo viene rasato in una trincea. Questa fotografia fa parte di una serie intitolata "La vita con i nostri alleati serbi", pubblicata in Gran Bretagna. I serbi erano considerati combattenti gentiluomini e alleati leali.

5. Air and sea
Por mar y aire
In cielo e in mare

A British battle squadron ploughs through an Atlantic swell,
September 1914. In the foreground are the guns of HMS
Audacious. Britannia, it appears, still rules the waves.

Un escuadrón de la marina británica atraviesa el Atlántico, en
septiembre de 1914. En primer plano aparecen los cañones del
Audacious. Como decía la canción, por aquel entonces, Gran
Bretaña todavía era "la reina de los mares".

Una squadra della marina britannica solca l'Atlantico, settembre
1914. In primo piano appaiono i cannoni dell' *Audacious*. Come
diceva la canzone, in quest'epoca la Gran Bretagna era ancora
"la regina dei mari".

5. Air and sea
Por mar y aire
In cielo e in mare

The First World War was a turning point in the history of naval warfare. For close on a hundred years the British navy had been seen by many as a global police force that patrolled the oceans, making sure that the *Pax Britannica* was rigorously enforced. In the years leading up to 1914, however, the German navy had reached near parity in size and strength. During the four long years of war the two fleets risked confrontation only once, at Jutland in 1916. Thereafter Germany relied on the submarine to rule beneath the waves.

The new player soaring high above the field of battle was the plane. The best means of observation and communication, it struck terror into the hearts of civilians and infuriated the dying breed of cavalry generals. Its supporters went perhaps a little too far in extolling its military virtues. Jan Smuts, a member of Lloyd George's War Cabinet, and Hugh Montague Trenchard (first officer commanding the Royal Flying Corps) believed that, given enough planes, total victory could be achieved without the need for fighting on the ground.

That was never proved. But, in a war short of heroes, the fighting aces of France, the United States, Germany and Britain became as famous as film stars or footballers.

La Primera Guerra Mundial marcó un antes y un después en la historia de la guerra naval. Durante casi cien años, se había considerado la marina británica una especie de policía mundial que patrullaba los océanos, garantizando el cumplimiento escrupuloso de la *Pax Britannica*. Sin embargo, en los años anteriores a 1914 la marina alemana prácticamente la había igualado en tamaño y fuerza. Durante los cuatro largos años de guerra solo se arriesgaron a enfrentarse una vez, en Jutlandia, en 1916. A partir de entonces, Alemania confió en su flota submarina para dominar los mares.

El avión se convirtió en el nuevo protagonista capaz de elevarse muy por encima del campo de batalla. Era el mejor medio de observación y comunicación, sembraba el pánico entre los civiles y enfurecía a los generales de una caballería en vías de extinción. No cabe duda de que los defensores del avión exageraban sus virtudes militares. Jan Smuts, miembro del gabinete de guerra de Lloyd George, y Hugh Montague Trenchard (primer oficial de los Royal Flying Corps) consideraban que si disponían del número de aviones suficiente, podrían alcanzar la victoria total sin necesidad de luchar en tierra.

Dicha teoría nunca fue probada. Sin embargo, en una guerra en la que escaseaban los héroes, los ases del cielo, ya fueran franceses, estadounidenses, alemanes o británicos llegaron a ser tan famosos como las estrellas del cine o los futbolistas.

La Prima guerra mondiale costituì una svolta nella storia della guerra navale. Per più di cent'anni la marina britannica era stata considerata una sorta di polizia mondiale che controllava i mari, assicurando il rigoroso rispetto della Pax Britannica. Negli anni precedenti il 1914, tuttavia, la marina tedesca l'aveva quasi eguagliata, sia come numero che come potenza. Nei quattro lunghi anni della guerra, le due flotte rischiarono il confronto solo una volta, nello Jutland, nel 1916.

Da quel momento in poi, la Germania fece affidamento sulla sua flotta sottomarina per dominare i mari, e l'aereo divenne il protagonista sopra i campi di battaglia. Ideale per osservare e comunicare, seminava il terrore tra i civili e faceva infuriare gli ufficiali di cavalleria. I sostenitori dell'aviazione esageravano sicuramente quando evocavano le sue qualità militari. Jan Smuts, un membro del Gabinetto di guerra di Lloyd George, e Hugh Montague Trenchard (primo ufficiale al comando del Royal Flying Corps) ritenevano che con un numero sufficiente di aerei avrebbero ottenuto una vittoria totale senza guerra di terra.

Questa teoria non fu mai provata. Ma in una guerra con pochi eroi, i cavalieri del cielo, che si trattasse di francesi, americani, tedeschi o britannici, divennero famosi quanto star del cinema o calciatori odierni.

(Above) Eddie Rickenbacker at the controls of his French SPAD 13, 1917. Rickenbacker was the top US ace, with twenty-six kills. (Opposite) British SE-5s in a dogfight with German Fokker D7s, 1915.

(Arriba) Eddie Rickenbacker al mando de su SPAD 13 francés, en 1917. Rickenbacker era el mejor piloto estadounidense y había abatido 26 aviones. (Página siguiente) SE-5 británicos en pleno combate aéreo contra unos Fokker D7 alemanes, en 1915.

(Sopra) Eddie Rickenbacker pilota il suo SPAD 13 francese, 1917. Rickenbacker era il miglior pilota americano, con 26 aerei abbattuti al suo attivo. (Accanto) SE-5 britannici coinvolti in un combattimento aereo contro dei Fokker D7 tedeschi, 1915.

(Opposite) A German biplane drops a bomb, 1917. (Right) A German balloon drops an observer, 1918. He is parachuting to safety after the balloon has been hit.

(Página anterior) Un biplano alemán deja caer una bomba, en 1917. (Derecha) Un observador salta en paracaídas desde un globo alemán, en 1918. Trata de ponerse a salvo ya que el globo ha sido alcanzado.

(Accanto) Un biplano tedesco lancia una bomba, 1917. (A destra) Un osservatore salta da una mongolfiera tedesca colpita, 1918. Si salverà grazie al paracadute.

(Above) The crow's nest and foredeck of the USS *Kentucky*, January 1917. (Opposite) Sopwith 2F1 Camels on the deck of HMS *Furious*. These aircraft were flown from the carrier in July 1918 to bomb Zeppelins in their sheds at Tondern.

(Arriba) Plataforma del vigía y puente de proa del buque estadounidense *Kentucky*, en enero de 1917. (Página siguiente) Camels Sopwith 2F1 en el puente del buque británico *Furious*. Estos aviones despegaban del portaaviones para bombardear los zepelines en sus hangares de Tondern, en julio de 1918.

(Sopra) La coffa e il ponte di prua dell'USS *Kentucky*, gennaio 1917. (Accanto) Camel Sopwith 2F1 sul ponte del HMS *Furious*. Questi aerei decollavano dalle portaerei per bombardare gli Zeppelin degli hangar di Tondern, luglio 1918.

The German battle-cruiser *Blücher* moments before sinking off the Dogger Bank, 24 January 1915. Seven hundred sailors were drowned.

El crucero de combate alemán *Blücher,* momentos antes de hundirse en el Doggerbank, el 24 de enero de 1915. Setecientos marineros murieron ahogados.

La corazzata tedesca Blücher pochi minuti prima di affondare al largo di Dogger Bank, il 24 gennaio 1915. Settecento marinai morirono annegati.

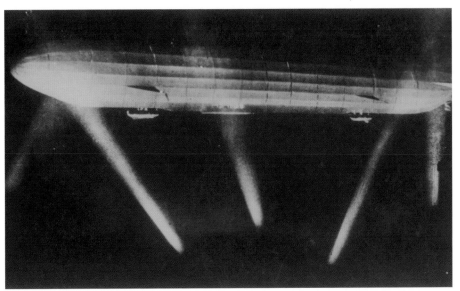

Measures taken against the menace of the Zeppelin raids. (Opposite) An apron hangs from balloons as part of London's air defences, 1915. (Above) Searchlights pick up a Zeppelin during a night raid, 1916.

Medidas para hacer frente a la amenaza de los ataques de los zepelines. (Página siguiente) Esta especie de red colgada de unos globos forma parte del sistema de defensa de Londres, en 1915. (Arriba) Los proyectores dan con un zepelín durante un ataque nocturno, 1916.

Provvedimenti per far fronte alla minaccia rappresentata dagli Zeppelin. (Accanto) Un 'grembiule' sospeso a dei palloni nel cielo di Londra fa parte dei sistemi di difesa aerea. (Sopra) I proiettori scoprono uno Zeppelin durante un raid notturno, 1916.

A hand-operated siren sounds the warning of an air-raid over the rooftops of Paris, 20 October 1917. London and Paris were the cities to suffer most from bombing raids during the war.

Una sirena accionada manualmente avisa de un ataque aéreo sobre los tejados de París, el 20 de octubre de 1917. Londres y París fueron las ciudades que más bombardeos sufrieron durante la guerra.

Sirena azionata manualmente per segnalare un raid aereo sui tetti di Parigi, 20 ottobre 1917. Durante la guerra Londra e Parigi furono le città più colpite dai bombardamenti aerei.

Remains of a Zeppelin at Potters Bar, Hertfordshire, 2 October 1916. 'Flames shot up from the top of the Zep and there were shouts and cheers…We all rushed out. The Zeppelin was all alight, falling like some burning firey star…' – from an eyewitness account.

Restos de un zepelín en Potters Bar, Hertfordshire, el 2 de octubre de 1916. "Las llamas surgían por encima del zepelín y se oían gritos. Todos salimos corriendo. El zepelín se había incendiado y caía como un meteorito en llamas…" declaró un testigo del suceso.

Resti di uno Zeppelin a Potters Bar (Hertfordshire), 2 ottobre 1916. "Nella parte superiore dello Zeppelin si vedevano delle fiamme, e si udivano grida ed esclamazioni. Tutti siamo usciti di corsa. Lo Zeppelin era in fiamme e cadeva come un meteorite…" racconta un testimone della scena.

A French aviator helps load bombs on to his biplane, 1 June 1915. Bombers had
a two-man crew. The bomber sat behind the pilot and simply dropped bombs
over the side of the plane.

Un aviador francés ayuda a cargar bombas en su biplano, el 1 de junio de 1915.
Los bombarderos estaban tripulados por dos hombres: el piloto y el encargado
de lanzar las bombas, que simplemente las dejaba caer por uno de los lados del
aparato.

Un aviatore francese aiuta a caricare delle bombe sul suo biplano, 1° giugno
1915. L'equipaggio dei bombardieri era formato da due persone. Il bombardiere,
seduto dietro al pilota, semplicemente gettava le bombe dal lato dell'aereo.

The body of a German pilot, 1916. Before the invention of the parachute, there was nothing that could be done to escape from a crippled plane. Senior officers opposed the use of the parachute, claiming it would encourage cowardice in action.

Cadáver de un piloto alemán, en 1916. Antes de inventarse el paracaídas, no había ningún medio de escapar de un avión alcanzado. Los oficiales superiores se oponían al uso del paracaídas ya que, según ellos, fomentaba los actos de cobardía.

Il corpo di un pilota tedesco, 1916. Fino all'invenzione del paracadute, non era possibile sopravvivere a un incidente aereo. Gli ufficiali superiori si opponevano all'utilizzo del paracadute, in quanto ritenevano che favorisse gli atti di codardia.

Baron Manfred
von Richthofen
('The Red Baron')
returns to earth after
a reconnaissance
flight in his Albatross.

El barón Manfred
von Richthofen
(el Barón Rojo)
aterriza tras un vuelo
de reconocimiento
en su *Albatros*.

Il "Barone Rosso"
Manfred von
Richthofen di
ritorno da un volo
di ricognizione a
bordo del suo
Albatros.

Von Richthofen's famous 'Flying Circus' – the 11th Pursuit Squadron – on parade in a field in France, 1917. Von Richthofen died when he was shot down over the Somme on 22 April 1918. He was credited with eighty 'kills'.

El famoso "Circo Volante" de von Richthofen –la undécima escuadrilla de caza– en formación en un campo de Francia, en 1917. Von Richthofen murió el 22 de abril de 1918 mientras sobrevolaba el Somme tras ser abatido. Se decía que había derribado hasta 80 aviones enemigos.

Parata del celebre 'Flying Circus' di von Richthofen – l'undicesima squadriglia da caccia – su un campo francese, 1917. Von Richthofen morì in volo: il suo aereo fu colpito sulla Somma il 22 aprile 1918. Gli si attribuiscono 80 abbattimenti.

American pilots in flying gear await the call to arms in their tent at Toul, on
the Moselle, 6 October 1918. An almost identical picture could have been
taken twenty-five years later.

Pilotos estadounidenses con los trajes de vuelo esperan el aviso para entrar
en combate en su tienda de Toul, en la Moselle, el 6 de octubre de 1918.
Veinticinco años después podría haberse tomado una fotografía casi idéntica.

Piloti americani in tenuta di volo aspettano la chiamata alle armi nella loro
tenda a Toul, nella Moselle, il 6 ottobre 1918. Una foto quasi identica
avrebbe potuto essere scattata venticinque anni dopo.

A meeting between two arms of modern technology. A US army cameraman films the take-off of an American Nieuport 28 biplane in the summer of 1918. The tented hangar indicates that aerodromes were portable affairs.

Dos aplicaciones de la tecnología moderna. Un cámara del ejército estadounidense filma el despegue de un biplano Nieuport-28 en el verano de 1918. La tienda que servía de hangar revela que los aeródromos se instalaban en cualquier parte.

Incontro tra due armi della tecnologia moderna. Un cameraman americano filma il decollo di un biplano Nieuport 28 americano nell'estate del 1918. La tenda che fa da hangar indica che gli aeroporti venivano montati un po' ovunque.

Falling from the skies. The vertical landing of a British seaplane, 10 May 1917.
In machines made largely of wood and canvas, a pilot's chance of surviving a
crash was better over water than over land.

Caído del cielo. Aterrizaje vertical de un hidroavión británico, el 10 de mayo
de 1917. En unos aparatos hechos con madera y tela, había más posibilidades
de sobrevivir a un accidente si se caía en el agua que si se hacía en tierra firme.

Caduto dal cielo. Atterraggio verticale di un idrovolante britannico, 10 maggio
1917. Gli aerei erano fatti in gran parte di legno e tela, pertanto le possibilità
di sopravvivere di un pilota erano maggiori in acqua che sulla terraferma.

Steaming into action. A battleship comes under fire during the Battle of Jutland, 31 May 1916. Two hundred and fifty ships and twenty-five admirals clashed in a battle that lasted little more than ten minutes.

Entrada en combate. Un buque de guerra participa en la batalla de Jutlandia, el 31 de mayo de 1916. Un total de 250 barcos y 25 almirantes se enfrentaron en una batalla que duró poco más de diez minutos.

A pieno gas verso la battaglia. Un nave da guerra viene presa di mira nella battaglia dello Jutland, 31 maggio 1916. 250 navi e 25 ammiragli si scontrarono in una battaglia che durò poco più di dieci minuti.

One of the most feared weapons of the war – a German U-boat – surfaces, 1917. It was the year that Germany announced unrestricted submarine warfare, an action that provoked President Wilson into declaring the 'armed neutrality' of the USA.

Una de las armas más temidas de la guerra –un submarino alemán– emerge a la superficie, en 1917. Aquel año, Alemania anunció que se embarcaba en una guerra submarina sin cuartel, lo cual hizo que el presidente Wilson declarara la "neutralidad armada" de Estados Unidos.

Un sottomarino tedesco – una delle armi più temute di questa guerra – in emersione, 1917. Fu l'anno in cui la Germania annunciò la guerra navale illimitata, dichiarazione che fece proclamare al presidente Wilson "la neutralità armata" degli Stati Uniti.

The engine room of a U-boat, 1916. Though greatly feared, U-boats inflicted far less damage than the public were led to believe by the huge publicity that was given to U-boat 'kills'.

Sala de máquinas de un submarino, en 1916. Aunque eran muy temidos, los submarinos causaban mucho menos daño de lo que la gente imaginaba debido a la gran publicidad que se daba a sus ataques.

Sala macchine di un sottomarino, 1916. Benché fossero molto temuti, i sottomarini fecero molti meno danni rispetto alle aspettative create nella gente dall'enorme pubblicità fatta alla presunta pericolosità dei loro attacchi.

(Above) The team that built the US destroyer *Liberty* in only seventeen days poses for the camera on the day of her completion, 1917. (Opposite) A large crowd watches the launch of yet another American ship, 1918.

(Arriba) El equipo que construyó el destructor estadounidense *Liberty* en solo 17 días posa ante la cámara el día de su finalización, en 1917. (Página siguiente) Una multitud asiste a la botadura de otro buque estadounidense, en 1918.

(Sopra) La squadra che construì il destroyer americano *Liberty* in soli diciassette giorni posa per le camere, 1917. (Accanto) Un folla numerosa assiste al varo di un'altra nave americana, nel 1918.

6. Peace
La paz
La pace

Cheering crowds on a London bus greet the signing of the Armistice, 11 November 1918. At last the war was over – and in time for Christmas, though four years too late to save 10 million lives.

Una multitud entusiasta a bordo de un autobús londinense celebra la firma del armisticio, el 11 de noviembre de 1918. Por fin había terminado la guerra, a tiempo para celebrar la Navidad pero con cuatro años de retraso para salvar diez millones de vidas humanas.

Una folla entusiasta, in un autobus londinese, saluta la firma dell'Armistizio, l'11 novembre 1918. Finalmente la guerra è finita e prima di Natale, anche se troppo tardi per salvare 10 milioni di vite.

6. Peace
La paz
La pace

The guns finally stopped firing at the eleventh hour of the eleventh day of the eleventh month of 1918. On the Western Front there was no fraternisation and little rejoicing, just an intense degree of relief. Many veterans noted that within half an hour of the guns falling silent the birds began to sing again.

In Paris, New York and London, the moment was greeted more raucously. Workers poured out of shops and offices. Buses were commandeered, filled with soldiers, sailors and civilians and driven through thronging crowds to the city centres. Bonfires and fireworks illuminated parks, squares and avenues. People sang and danced, waved flags, collapsed in drunken joy. The celebrations continued for three days until police gradually restored order.

In Berlin, the Armistice was greeted with almost total silence. Ten-year-old Steffie Spira went with her sister to see the ragged, worn-out, dishevelled soldiers arriving at the Brandenburg Gate. 'It was a sad occasion – people cried… I gave a soldier my little bouquet and he said "Good luck to you, little miss." I will never forget the grief in his eyes.'

Los cañones enmudecieron, por fin, a las once de la mañana del día once del undécimo mes del año 1918. En el frente occidental no hubo ninguna escena de confraternización y muy pocas expresiones de alegría, tan solo una enorme sensación de alivio. Muchos veteranos afirmaron que media hora después de que callaran las armas los pájaros volvieron a trinar.

En París, Nueva York y Londres, el acontecimiento se celebró por todo lo alto. Los empleados salieron en masa de las tiendas y las oficinas. Se requisaron los autobuses, que se llenaron de soldados, marineros y civiles, y recorrieron los centros de las ciudades ante una multitud enfervorecida. Hogueras y fuegos artificiales iluminaron los parques, las plazas y las avenidas. La gente cantaba y bailaba, y agitaba banderas, embriagada de alegría. Las celebraciones duraron tres días hasta que la policía restableció el orden paulatinamente.

En Berlín, se acogió el armisticio con un silencio casi total. La pequeña Steffie Spira, de diez años de edad, asistió junto con su hermana al regreso de los soldados, quienes, andrajosos, agotados y despeinados cruzaban la puerta de Brandenburgo. "Fue muy triste … la gente lloraba… Le di mi ramito de flores a un soldado y me dijo 'buena suerte, pequeña'. Nunca olvidaré la tristeza de su mirada. "

I cannoni tacquero alle undici del mattino dell'undicesimo giorno dell'undicesimo mese del 1918. Sul fronte occidentale non vi furono scene di fraternizzazione e gioia, ma solo un gran senso di sollievo. Molti veterani notarono che un'ora dopo il cessate il fuoco gli uccelli avevano ripreso a cantare.

A Parigi, New York e Londra l'evento fu celebrato più rumorosamente. I dipendenti di negozi e uffici uscirono in strada. Gli autobus furono requisiti, riempiti di soldati, marinai e civili e guidati tra la folla acclamante verso il centro città. Falò e fuochi d'artificio illuminarono i parchi, le piazze e i viali. La gente cantava e ballava, agitava bandiere, si ubriacava. I festeggiamenti continuarono per tre giorni prima che la polizia riportasse gradualmente l'ordine.

A Berlino, l'armistizio venne accolto con un silenzio quasi totale. Steffie Spira, di dieci anni, assistette con sua sorella al ritorno dei soldati con gli abiti strappati, le barbe lunghe e l'aria stremata presso la Porta di Brandeburgo. "Era triste… La gente piangeva… Ho dato un mazzetto di fiori a un soldato e lui mi ha detto "Buona fortuna, signorina". Non dimenticherò mai la tristezza del suo sguardo."

(Above) Anticipating the event. On 4 October 1918, the crew of the *Victory* parade to spell out the name of their ship and their goal. (Opposite) At Camp Sherman, Ohio, 21,000 officers and soldiers form the head of President Wilson, 1918.

(Arriba) Anticipándose al acontecimiento. El 4 de octubre de 1918, la tripulación del *Victory* desfila formando las letras de su barco y de su objetivo. (Página siguiente) En Camp Sherman, Ohio, 21.000 oficiales y soldados forman la cabeza del presidente Wilson, en 1918.

(Accanto) Anticipazione. Il 4 ottobre 1918, l'equipaggio del *Victory* sfila formando le lettere della nave e del suo obiettivo. (Accanto) A Camp Sherman (Ohio), 21.000 ufficiali e soldati si unirono per formare la testa del Presidente Wilson, 1918.

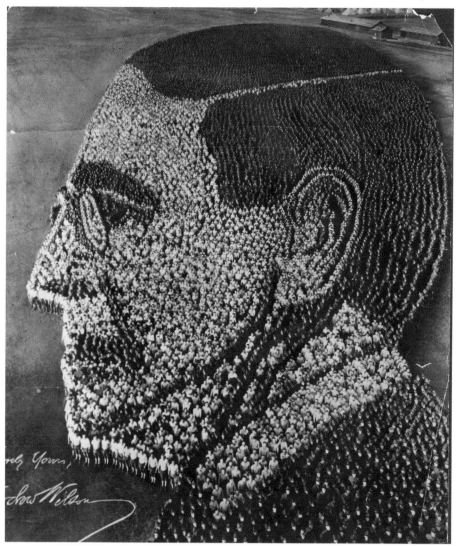

Tens of thousands of Londoners gather in Trafalgar Square to celebrate the signing of the Peace Treaty at Versailles, June 1919. The War to End All Wars was finally and irrevocably over.

Decenas de miles de londinenses se congregan en Trafalgar Square para celebrar la firma del Tratado de Paz de Versalles, en junio de 1919. La Gran Guerra, la que debía marcar el final de todas las guerras, había terminado por fin.

Decine di migliaia di londinesi si riuniscono a Trafalgar Square per celebrare la firma del Trattato di Versailles, giugno 1919. La Grande Guerra, che doveva essere l'ultima, era definitivamente e irrevocabilmente finita.

Happy and affluent. One of the tables of merrymakers at the Ritz Hotel, London, November 1918. At the Savoy, according to Noël Coward: 'Everybody wore paper caps, and threw streamers, and drank champagne and sang the *Marseillaise…*'

Felices y prósperos. Una mesa de juerguistas en el Hotel Ritz, Londres, en noviembre de 1918. En el Savoy, según Noël Coward, "todo el mundo se ponía sombreros de papel, tiraba serpentinas, bebía champán y cantaba La Marsellesa… ".

Ricchi e felici. Un'allegra tavolata all'Hotel Ritz di Londres, novembre 1918. Al Savoy, secondo Noel Coward, "tutti portavano berrettini di carta, tiravano stelle filanti e bevevano champagne cantando la Marsigliese…".

Street of sorrow – Berlin in the immediate post-war period. People who had spent the last three years surviving on less than 1,000 calories a day now faced hunger, poverty, squalor and revolution.

Tristeza en las calles. Berlín, en la posguerra inmediata. Tras haber sobrevivido tres años con menos de 1.000 calorías diarias, la gente debe hacer frente al hambre, la pobreza, la miseria y la revolución.

Una strada piena di tristezza – Berlino nell'immediato dopoguerra. Dopo tre anni con meno di 1000 calorie al giorno, adesso la gente deve fare i conti con la fame, la povertà, lo squallore e la rivoluzione.

Street of joy – the East End of London at much the same time. 'Victory' parties were organised everywhere in the spring and summer of 1919 to celebrate the triumph of life over death.

Alegría en las calles. El East End londinense aproximadamente en el mismo momento. En la primavera y el verano de 1919 se organizaron numerosas fiestas de la "victoria" para celebrar el triunfo de la vida sobre la muerte.

Una strada piena di allegria – l'East End di Londra nello stesso periodo o quasi. Delle feste della "vittoria" furono organizzate ovunque durante la primavera e l'estate del 1919 per celebrare il trionfo della vita sulla morte.

The caricature Kaiser. A crowd of revellers celebrates the Armistice in London, 11 November 1918.
The caption to the drawing reads: 'Gone to a better [h]ole', a reference to a famous First World War
cartoon by Bruce Bairnsfather.

Caricatura del káiser. Unos juerguistas celebran el armisticio en Londres, el 11 de noviembre de
1918. La leyenda del dibujo reza: "Huyó a esconderse en un agujero mejor" y hace referencia a
una caricatura realizada por Bruce Bairnsfather durante la Primera Guerra Mundial.

Caricatura del Kaiser. Un gruppo festeggia l'Armistizio a Londra, l'11 novembre 1918. La didascalia
del disegno recita: 'Gone to a better [h]ole', in riferimento a un celebre disegno umoristico di Bruce
Bairnsfather durante la Prima guerra mondiale.

The real Kaiser. His Imperial Highness the Emperor Wilhelm II of Germany in the gardens of his home in the Netherlands following his abdication and exile, 28 December 1918. A month earlier he had exclaimed: 'It's just that damned Berlin that's against me!'

El auténtico káiser. Su alteza imperial, el káiser Guillermo II de Alemania en los jardines de su residencia en los Países Bajos tras abdicar y exiliarse, el 28 de noviembre de 1918. Un mes antes, había afirmado: "¡Lo único que está en mi contra es ese condenado Berlín!".

Il vero imperatore. Sua Altezza l'imperatore Guglielmo II di Germania nei giardini della sua dimora nei Paesi Bassi dove si esiliò dopo aver abdicato il 28 dicembre del 1918. Un mese prima aveva esclamato: "Solo questa maledetta Berlino è contro di me!".

The German delegates arrive at the Versailles Peace Conference, led by the Foreign Minister, Ulrich Graf von Brockdorff-Rantzau, 7 May 1919. It was the day that the Peace Treaty was first handed to the Germans.

Llegada de los delegados alemanes a la Conferencia de Paz de Versalles, encabezados por el ministro de Asuntos Exteriores, Ulrich Graf von Brockdorff-Rantzau, el 7 de mayo de 1919. Aquel fue el día en que se entregó el tratado de paz por primera vez a los alemanes.

I delegati tedeschi arrivano al congresso di Versailles, capitanati dal ministro degli Esteri, Ulrich Graf von Brockdorff-Rantzau, il 7 maggio 1919. È il giorno in cui il Trattato di pace viene reso noto ai tedeschi.

The Allied triumvirate arrives at Versailles, 1 June 1919 – (from left to right) Georges Clémenceau, Prime Minister of France; Woodrow Wilson, President of the USA; and Lloyd George, the British Prime Minister.

El triunvirato de aliados a su llegada a Versailles, el 1 de junio de 1919. (De izquierda a derecha) Georges Clémenceau, primer ministro francés, Woodrow Wilson, presidente de Estados Unidos, y Lloyd George, primer ministro británico.

Il triumvirato degli Alleati al suo arrivo a Versailles, il 1º giugno 1919. Da sinistra a destra, Georges Clémenceau, Primo ministro francese, Woodrow Wilson, Presidente degli Stati Uniti, e Lloyd George, Primo ministro britannico.

Allied officers peer through the windows into the
Hall of Mirrors to witness the signing of the Peace Treaty,
28 June 1919. The German delegation had no choice. Had
they refused to sign, Germany would have been invaded.

Los oficiales aliados asisten, a través de las ventanas de
la Sala de los Espejos, a la firma del Tratado de Paz, el 28
de junio de 1919. La delegación alemana no tuvo elección.
De haberse negado a firmarlo, las potencias aliadas habrían
invadido Alemania.

Gli ufficiali alleati assistono attraverso le vetrate della Sala
degli Specchi alla firma del Trattato di pace, il 28 giugno
1919. La delegazione tedesca non ha scelta. Se si rifiuta
di firmare, la Germania verrà invasa.

A member of the German air force cuts up a pile of airmen's helmets, 1919. Under the terms of the Treaty of Versailles, Germany was compelled to destroy almost all military weapons and equipment.

Un soldado del ejército del aire alemán corta en pedazos cascos de piloto, en 1919. Según lo estipulado por el Tratado de Versalles, Alemania debía destruir casi todas las armas y los equipos militares de que disponía.

Un soldato dell'aviazione tedesca distrugge dei caschi da pilota, 1919. Secondo il Trattato di Versailles, la Germania era obbligata a distruggere la quasi totalità delle sue armi e attrezzature militari.

A tank is dismembered on the outskirts of Berlin, 1919. Although the
machine bears the German insignia, it was in fact a British tank, captured
on the Western Front late in the war.

Desmantelamiento de un tanque en las afueras de Berlín, en 1919.
Aunque la máquina lleva la insignia alemana, en realidad es un tanque
británico aprehendido en el frente occidental hacia el final de la guerra.

Un carro armato viene smantellato nei pressi di Berlino, 1919. Benché
la macchina mostri l'insegna tedesca, di fatto si tratta di un carro armato
britannico, requisito sul fronte occidentale verso la fine della guerra.

The German High Seas Fleet surrenders to Admiral Beatty in the cold waters of
Scapa Flow in the Orkney Islands, Scotland, 21 November 1918. It had never
before been defeated in battle.

La flota alemana de alta mar se rinde al almirante Beatty en las gélidas aguas
de Scapa Flow en las islas Orkney, Escocia, el 21 de noviembre de 1918. Hasta
entonces, se había mantenido invicta.

La flotta tedesca di alto mare si arrende all'ammiraglio Beatty nelle fredde acque
di Scapa Flow, nelle isole Orkney (Scozia), il 21 novembre 1918. Fino ad allora
non era mai stata sconfitta.

Viscount Curzon, a member of Lloyd George's War Cabinet, films the surrender of the
German fleet at Scapa Flow. Seven months later, the ships were scuttled by their crews,
in protest against the terms of the Treaty of Versailles.

El vizconde Curzon, miembro del gabinete de guerra de Lloyd George, filma la rendición
de la flota alemana en Scapa Flow. Siete meses después, las propias tripulaciones
hundieron los buques en protesta por las condiciones del Tratado de Versalles.

Il visconte Curzon, un membro del gabinetto di guerra di Lloyd George, filma la resa della
flotta tedesca a Scapa Flow. Sette mesi dopo, le navi furono affondate dagli equipaggi per
protestare contro il Trattato di Versailles.

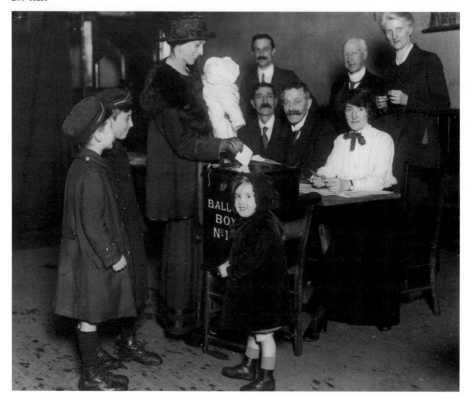

One of the fruits of victory – a newly-enfranchised woman votes for the
first time in a British Parliamentary election, 14 December 1918. Women
over 30 years of age had been given the vote.

Uno de los frutos de la victoria: esta mujer vota por primera vez durante
las elecciones al Parlamento británico, el 14 de diciembre de 1918. Se
reconoció el derecho al voto a las mujeres mayores de 30 años.

Uno dei frutti della vittoria: questa donna vota per la prima volta in
occasione delle elezioni del Parlamento britannico, il 14 dicembre 1918.
Il diritto di voto era stato accordato alle donne di più di 30 anni.

Nancy Witcher Langhorne, Viscountess Astor, with her husband William Waldorf Astor, campaigns for the Conservative Party in Plymouth during the 1919 election. Although born in the United States, she became the first woman MP in Britain.

Nancy Witcher Langhorne, vizcondesa de Astor, con su marido William Waldorf Astor, en plena campaña a favor del Partido Conservador en Plymouth, en 1919. A pesar de que había nacido en Estados Unidos, fue la primera mujer diputada del Parlamento británico.

La viscontessa di Astor, Nancy Witcher Langhorne, accompagnata dal marito William Waldorf Astor, fa campagna elettorale per il partito conservatore a Plymouth, in occasione delle elezioni del 1919. Benché fosse nata negli Stati Uniti, fu la prima donna eletta deputato al Parlamento britannico.

7. Revolution
La revolución
La rivoluzione

'We shall now proceed to construct the socialist order...' Vladimir Ilyich Lenin addresses a crowd, 1917. Lenin was the architect, midwife and guiding spirit of the Bolshevik Revolution.

"Ahora debemos instaurar el orden socialista... " declaró Vladimir Illich Lenin a la multitud, en 1917. Lenin fue el arquitecto, el partero y el guía espiritual de la revolución bolchevique.

"Adesso procederemo a instaurare l'ordine socialista..." dichiara Ilyich Lenin alla folla nel 1917. Lenin fu l'architetto, la levatrice e la guida spirituale della Rivoluzione bolscevica.

7. Revolution
   La revolución
   La rivoluzione

In the restless years from 1910 to 1919 revolution raised its spitting, snarling head all over the world. There were revolutions and rebellions in Nicaragua and Mexico. Portugal erupted in violence in October 1910, forcing King Manuel II to make his way hastily to Gibraltar. Ulster spluttered and threatened civil war in 1913. Dublin broke out in armed insurrection three years later. The vicissitudes of war proved too much for the peoples of the old empires of Europe. In October 1918 the Austro-Hungarian Empire disintegrated.

Within the next few months there were revolutions in Germany and Hungary. Berlin was the centre of German discontent. Democrats, Communists, and members of the *Freikorps* clashed on the streets. Horrendous killings took place against a background of poverty, starvation and economic depression.

But the most shattering of all was the Russian Revolution. Imperial Russia was overthrown by a crescendo of risings and protests that culminated in the Bolshevik coup of November 1917. The Tsar and his family, whose public glory had been matched by their private sadness, were taken by Red Guards to Yekaterinburg, where they were shot in July 1918. The rule of the Romanovs had come to a bitter and bloody end.

Durante los años de agitación que fueron de 1910 a 1919, el rostro amenazador de la revolución estuvo presente en todo el mundo. Hubo revoluciones y rebeliones en Nicaragua y México. La violencia estalló en Portugal en octubre de 1910 y obligó al rey Manuel II a huir a Gibraltar. En el Ulster, el clima se tornó explosivo y en 1913 la guerra civil acechaba. En Dublín estalló una insurrección armada tres años después. Las vicisitudes de la guerra resultaron insalvables para la población de los antiguos imperios del viejo continente y el imperio austrohúngaro acabó desintegrándose en octubre de 1918.

En los meses posteriores, estallaron revoluciones en Alemania y Hungría. Berlín fue el centro del descontento alemán. Demócratas, comunistas y miembros de los *Freikorps* se enfrentaban en las calles. Se produjeron horrendos asesinatos ante un telón de fondo dominado por la pobreza, el hambre y la crisis económica.

Pero la revolución rusa fue la más terrible de todas. La Rusia imperial se desmoronó tras una serie de levantamientos y manifestaciones que culminaron con el golpe de estado bolchevique de noviembre de 1917. El zar y su familia, cuya gloria pública era equiparable a su tristeza privada, fueron llevados por la Guardia Roja a Yekaterimburgo y ejecutados en julio de 1918. De ese modo el reinado de los Romanov llegó a un amargo y sangriento fin.

Negli anni senza pace tra il 1910 e il 1919, la rivoluzione fece la sua comparsa in tutto il mondo. Ci furono sommosse e ribellioni in Nicaragua e in Messico. Il Portogallo piombò nella violenza nell'ottobre del 1910, obbligando il re Manuel II a fuggire a Gibilterra. In Ulster il clima divenne esplosivo e nel 1913 la guerra civile era imminente. Tre anni dopo, Dublino prese le armi. Le vicissitudini della guerra furono troppo dure per i popoli dei vecchi imperi europei e, nell'ottobre del 1918, l'Impero austro-ungarico si disintegrò.

Nei mesi successivi, la rivoluzione scoppiò in Germania e in Ungheria. Berlino fu il centro dello scontento tedesco. I democratici, i comunisti e i membri del Freikorps si scontrarono per strada. Stragi orrende ebbero luogo in uno scenario di povertà, fame e crisi economica.

Ma la rivoluzione russa fu la più sconvolgente. La Russia imperiale fu rovesciata da una serie di rivolte e manifestazioni che culminarono nel colpo di stato bolscevico del novembre del 1917. Lo zar e la sua famiglia, la cui gloria pubblica era pari solo alla tristezza privata, furono condotti dalla Guardia Rossa a Yekaterinburg e giustiziati nel luglio del 1918. Il regno dei Romanov finì amaramente e nel sangue.

The Big Three of the
Revolution. (Left to
right) Joseph Stalin,
Lenin and Mikhail
Ivanovich Kalinin at
the Congress of the
Russian Communist
Party, March 1919.

Las tres figuras de
la revolución. (De
izquierda a derecha)
Joseph Stalin, Lenin
y Mijaíl Ivanovich
Kalinin en el
congreso del Partido
Comunista ruso,
en marzo de 1919.

I tre grandi della
Rivoluzione. Da
sinistra a destra,
Stalin, Lenin e
Mikhaïl Ivanovitch
Kalinin al
Congresso del
Partito Comunista
russo, marzo 1919.

The siege of the Duma, July 1917. Crowds flee as fighting erupts between Bolsheviks and supporters of Alexander Kerensky's provisional government in the Nevsky Prospect, Petrograd (St Petersburg).

El asedio de la Duma, en julio de 1917. La multitud huye cuando estallan los enfrentamientos entre los bolcheviques y los partidarios del gobierno provisional de Alexander Kerensky en Nevsky Prospect, Petrogrado (San Petersburgo).

La sede della Duma, luglio 1917. La folla fugge mentre iniziano gli scontri sulla Prospettiva Nevsky a Petrograd (San Pietroburgo) tra bolscevichi e sostenitori del governo provvisorio di Alexander Kerensky.

Marines and members of the Red Guard prepare to attack the Winter Palace in Petrograd, October 1917. 'This is only a preliminary step toward a similar revolution everywhere' – Lenin.

Soldados de la infantería de marina y miembros de la Guardia Roja se preparan para atacar el Palacio de Invierno de Petrogrado, en octubre de 1917. "Este es solo el primer paso de una revolución que será similar en todo el mundo" –Lenin.

I marinai e i membri della Guardia Rossa si preparano ad attaccare il palazzo d'Inverno a Petrograd, ottobre 1917. "È solo il primo passo verso una rivoluzione che si estenderà ovunque" – Lenin.

Demonstrators outside the Winter Palace in
Petrograd, 1917. Kerensky fled to Moscow.
The days of the 'moderates' were numbered.

Manifestantes ante el Palacio de Invierno de
Petrogrado, en 1917. Kerensky huye a Moscú.
Los "moderados" tienen los días contados.

Manifestanti davanti al palazzo d'Inverno a
Petrogrado, 1917. Kerensky fugge a Mosca.
I giorni dei "moderati" sono contati.

'Where force is necessary, one should make use of it boldly.' Leon Trotsky,
newly-appointed Commissar for Foreign Affairs, watches Bolshevik troops
parade in Red Square, Moscow, 1918.

"Cuando es necesario recurrir a la fuerza, hay que hacerlo con decisión."
Leon Trotsky, el comisario de Asuntos Exteriores, asiste a un desfile de
las tropas bolcheviques en la Plaza Roja de Moscú, en 1918.

"Quando è necessario ricorrere alla forza, bisogna utilizzarla con coraggio".
Leone Trotsky, appena nominato commissario per gli Esteri, assiste alla
sfilata delle truppe bolsceviche sulla Piazza Rossa, Mosca, 1918.

A year earlier and a thousand miles to the west – Alexander Kerensky, Minister of War and leader of the provisional government, reviews Russian troops leaving for the Eastern Front, 1917.

Un año antes y a más de mil kilómetros al oeste, Alexander Kerensky, ministro de la Guerra y líder del Gobierno provisional, pasa revista a las tropas rusas que parten hacia el frente oriental, en 1917.

Un anno prima e un migliaio di chilometri più a ovest, Alexander Kerensky, ministro della Guerra e dirigente del governo provvisorio, passa in rivista le truppe russe pronte a partire per il fronte orientale, 1917.

(Above) Red Guards on the eve of the Bolshevik Revolution, October 1917. (Opposite) Members of the Russian royal family on the roof of the conservatory at Tobolsk, 1918 – (left to right) the Grand Duchesses Olga and Anastasia, the Tsar and Tsarevich, and the Grand Duchesses Tatiana and Marie.

(Arriba) Soldados de la Guardia Roja durante la víspera de la revolución bolchevique, en octubre de 1917. (Página siguiente) Miembros de la familia real rusa en el tejado del conservatorio de Tobolsk, en 1918. (De izquierda a derecha) Las grandes duquesas Olga y Anastasia, el zar y el zarevich, y las grandes duquesas Tatiana y María.

(Sopra) Soldati della Guardia Rossa alla vigilia della rivoluzione bolscevica, ottobre 1917. (Accanto) Membri della famiglia reale russa sul tetto del conservatorio a Tobolsk, 1918. Da sinistra a destra: le granduchesse Olga e Anastasia, lo zar, lo zarevic e le granduchesse Tatiana e Maria.

Daughters of the Tsar. (From left to right) The Grand Duchesses Marie, Tatiana, Anastasia and Olga in the happier days of 1914. All of them lost their lives at Yekaterinburg.

Las hijas del zar. (De izquierda a derecha) Las grandes duquesas María, Tatiana, Anastasia y Olga en los días felices de 1914. Todas fueron ejecutadas en Yekaterimburgo.

Le figlie dello zar. Da sinistra a destra: le granduchesse Maria, Tatiana, Anastasia e Olga negli anni felici, 1914. Tutte persero la vita a Yekaterinburg.

Daughters of the Revolution. Female Russian soldiers, 11 August 1917. Although originally recruited to fight alongside male troops in the Tsar's army, many brigades of women soldiers fought for the Bolshevik Revolution.

Las hijas de la revolución y mujeres soldados rusas, el 11 de agosto de 1917. Aunque fueron reclutadas originalmente para luchar junto a los hombres del ejército del zar, muchas brigadas de mujeres soldados se posicionaron a favor de la revolución bolchevique.

Le figlie della Rivoluzione. Donne soldato, 11 agosto 1917. Reclutate inizialmente per combattere a fianco dei soldati dell'esercito dello zar, molte di esse appoggiarono invece la Rivoluzione bolscevica.

Crowds run for safety as fighting breaks out in the Nevsky Prospect, Petrograd, October 1917.
'It remains to be seen whether Petrograd will be followed by the rest of Russia' wrote Arthur
Ransome, Foreign Correspondent of the *Daily News*. It was.

La multitud se dispersa a la carrera para escapar de las balas en Nevsky Prospect, Petrogrado,
en octubre de 1917. "¿Seguirá el resto de Rusia el ejemplo de Petrogrado?" escribió Arthur
Ransome, corresponsal en el extranjero del *Daily News*. En efecto, así sucedió.

La folla si disperde allo scoppio degli scontri sulla Prospettiva Nevsky a Petrograd, ottobre
1917. "Resta da vedere se tutta la Russia seguirà l'esempio di Petrograd" scrisse Arthur
Ransome, corrispondente del *Daily News*. Così fu.

Fighting on the streets of Berlin between government troops of Friedrich Ebert and the Spartacists, 1919. The Spartacists were mainly armed Communists and their supporters striving for a Socialist order.

Enfrentamientos en las calles de Berlín entre soldados del Gobierno de Friedrich Ebert y espartaquistas, en 1919. Los espartaquistas eran un grupo integrado fundamentalmente por el brazo armado del consumismo y por sus defensores, los cuales pretendían establecer un orden socialista.

Scontri per le strade di Berlino tra i soldati del governo di Friedrich Ebert e gli spartachisti, 1919. La maggioranza degli spartachisti erano comunisti armati che volevano instaurare un ordine socialista.

On 4 January 1919, Spartacists closed down Berlin's factories, power stations and public transport. They also occupied and raided most newspaper offices. (Above) Spartacists burn pamphlets and papers.

El 4 de enero de 1919, los espartaquistas cerraron las fábricas, las centrales eléctricas y los transportes públicos de Berlín. También ocuparon y asaltaron la mayoría de las sedes de los periódicos. (Arriba) Un grupo de espartaquistas quema panfletos.

Il 4 gennaio 1919, gli spartachisti fermarono le fabbriche, le centrali elettriche e i trasporti pubblici di Berlino, e occuparono e saccheggiarono la maggior parte delle redazioni dei giornali. (Sopra) Spartachisti bruciano riviste e libelli.

The Red Flag is carried through Berlin streets, December 1918. Troops joined the Spartacists when rumours spread of a right-wing counter-revolution. The rising lasted barely two months.

La bandera roja se exhibe por las calles de Berlín, en diciembre de 1918. Los soldados se unieron a los espartaquistas cuando se extendieron los rumores de que iba a producirse una contrarrevolución de derechas. El levantamiento apenas duró dos meses.

La bandiera rossa percorre le strade di Berlino, dicembre 1918. I soldati si schierarono con gli spartachisti quando si sparse la notizia di una possibile controrivoluzione di destra. Il sollevamento durò appena due mesi.

Rosa Luxemburg, the Polish-born co-founder of the Spartacist movement, 15 January 1919. It was the day of her arrest by counter-revolutionary volunteers. Hours later she was brutally murdered by them 'while attempting to escape'.

Rosa Luxemburg, nacida en Polonia y cofundadora del movimiento espartaquista, el 15 de enero de 1919. Ese mismo día fue arrestada por contrarrevolucionarios voluntarios, quienes la asesinaron brutalmente horas más tarde "cuando trataba de huir".

Rosa Luxemburg, cofondatrice del movimento spartachista, di origine polacca, fotografata il 15 gennaio 1919, nel giorno del suo arresto da parte dei controrivoluzionari. Qualche ora più tardi verrà brutalmente assassinata "mentre cerca di fuggire".

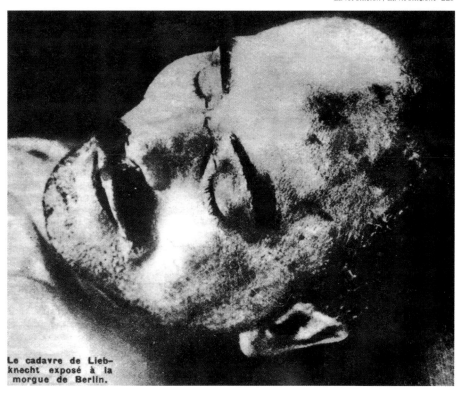

Le cadavre de Lieb-
knecht exposé à la
morgue de Berlín.

The corpse of Karl Liebknecht, co-founder of the Spartacists and leader of the party, 15 January 1919. The car carrying Liebknecht to Moabit Prison pulled up at the side of a dark road. Liebknecht was shot.

Cadáver de Karl Liebknecht, cofundador y dirigente del partido espartaquista, el 15 de enero de 1919. El coche que llevaba a Liebknecht a la cárcel de Moabit se paró en una calle poco iluminada y Liebknecht cayó abatido por las balas.

Il corpo di Karl Liebknecht, cofondatore e dirigente del partito spartachista, il 15 gennaio 1919. L'automobile che transportava Liebknecht alla prigione di Moabit si fermò sul ciglio di una strada oscura e Liebknecht fu assassinato.

8. Work
   Trabajo
   Lavoro

At the height of the war, women employees of the London
and North West Railway practise their skills in a typewriting
class, December 1917. The smiles to the camera were almost
certainly genuine.

En plena guerra, trabajadoras de los ferrocarriles de Londres
y del noroeste aprenden a escribir a máquina, en diciembre de
1917. Las sonrisas que dedican a la cámara seguramente son
sinceras.

Nel momento culminante della guerra, le dipendenti delle
ferrovie di Londra e del Nord-Ovest si allenano a scrivere a
macchina durante una lezione di dattilografia, dicembre 1917.
I loro sorrisi sono quasi sicuramente sinceri.

8.   Work
Trabajo
Lavoro

Industrially, it should have been the best of times. Order books were full for coal, steel, textiles, ships and armaments. New industries were expanding; indeed, the demand for motor cars seemed inexhaustible. Wages had never been higher. In January 1914, Henry Ford offered his workers $5 a day and (except for women) a profit-sharing scheme. In 1912 the *Code du Travail* was issued in France, standardising hours and wages. In the USA, the federal government moved towards establishing an eight-hour working day.

But the workplace became increasingly a place of strife, turmoil and tragedy. Britain was hit by a series of bitter disputes involving miners, dockers and railwaymen. In America, the IWW backed strikes by textile workers in Lawrence, Massachusetts, in 1912, and four years later more than three hundred IWW members were gaoled following a miners' strike at Scranton, Pennsylvania.

Women experienced the greatest changes at work. In the war they drove buses, delivered coal, ran sections of the railway systems, became police officers, soldiers, sailors and farm-workers. For millions of women such jobs were more exciting, more enjoyable and more profitable than anything that had gone before.

En lo que concierne a la industria, aquella época debía haber sido la mejor de todas. Los pedidos de carbón, acero, productos textiles, barcos y armamento se dispararon. Nuevos sectores experimentaban una expansión y el del automóvil, en concreto, parecía inagotable. Los salarios nunca habían sido tan elevados. En enero de 1914, Henry Ford ofrecía a sus trabajadores 5 dólares al día y (excepto a las mujeres) una participación en los beneficios. En 1912 apareció en Francia el *Code du travail* que establecía unos estándares de horas de trabajo y salarios. En Estados Unidos el Gobierno federal estaba a punto de instaurar la jornada de ocho horas.

Pero el lugar de trabajo pasó a ser escenario de conflicto, agitación y tragedia. Gran Bretaña se vio afectada por una serie de amargas disputas en las que participaron mineros, estibadores y ferroviarios. En Estados Unidos, el sindicato IWW apoyó las huelgas de los obreros del sector textil en Lawrence, Massachusetts, en 1912, y cuatro años después, más de 300 miembros de IWW fueron encarcelados tras una huelga de mineros en Scranton, Pennsylvania.

Las mujeres experimentaron los cambios más importantes en el trabajo. Durante la guerra, conducían autobuses, repartían carbón, supervisaban secciones de la red ferroviaria, se convirtieron en policías, soldados, marineras y granjeras. Para millones de mujeres, esos trabajos eran más entretenidos y rentables que los que habían realizado hasta entonces.

In campo industriale, quest'epoca avrebbe dovuto essere la migliore. I libri degli ordini erano pieni, che si trattasse di carbone, acciaio, tessuti, navi o armi. Si sviluppavano industrie nuove e il mercato dell'automobile sembrava inesauribile. I salari non erano mai stati così alti. Nel gennaio del 1914, Henry Ford offrì a suoi operai una remunerazione di 5 dollari al giorno nonché un programma di partecipazione ai profitti (non accessibile alle donne). Nel 1912 venne pubblicato in Francia il Codice del Lavoro, che armonizzava gli orari e i salari. Negli Stati Uniti, il governo federale stava per ratificare la giornata di otto ore.

Ma il mondo del lavoro divenne sempre più spesso un terreno di scontro, a volte drammatico. La Gran Bretagna fu colpita da una serie di conflitti che coinvolsero minatori, portuali e ferrovieri. Negli Stati Uniti, nel 1912, il sindacato IWW appoggiò gli scioperi delle operaie del tessile a Lawrence, ma quattro anni dopo, nel 1918, più di 300 membri del IWW furono incarcerati in seguito a uno sciopero di minatori a Scranton, in Pennsylvania.

Nel lavoro furono le donne a sperimentare i maggiori cambiamenti. Durante la guerra iniziarono a condurre autobus, trasportare carbone, gestire linee ferroviarie; divennero agenti di polizia, soldatesse o operaie agricole. Per le donne, questi impieghi erano molto più interessanti e redditizi delle mansioni svolte fino a quel momento.

(Opposite) Out with the old… the driver of a horse-drawn tram. (Right) …and in with the new – the driver of an electric tram.

(Página anterior) Adiós a lo viejo… el conductor de un tranvía tirado por caballos. (Derecha) … y bienvenido lo nuevo (el conductor de un tranvía eléctrico).

(Accanto) Basta col passato… e con i conducenti dei tramtrainati dai cavalli. (A destra) Il nuovo avanza… il conducente di un tram elettrico.

(Left) Releasing the brake – a London bus driver, March 1910. (Opposite) Releasing the slip coach – a guard on a LNWR train detaches the rear car.

(Izquierda) Soltando el freno; conductor de un autobús londinense, en marzo de 1910. (Página siguiente) Soltando un vagón. Un ferroviario londinense procede a soltar el vagón de cola.

(A sinistra) Rilasciando il freno – il conducente di un autobus londinese, marzo 1910. (Accanto) Sganciando un vagone – un agente delle ferrovie londinesi stacca un vagone da un convoglio.

(Opposite) A conductress on an open-top bus, 1916. (Above) The guard on a Metropolitan train, north London, 28 December 1916. The boots may well have warmed the heart of many a commuter on this cold grey day…

(Página anterior) Conductora de un autobús descubierto, en 1916. (Arriba) Una agente del metro, en el norte de Londres, 28 de diciembre de 1916. Es probable que su atuendo hiciera entrar en calor a más de un pasajero aquel día frío y gris.

(Accanto) Un controllore donna sulla piattaforma scoperta di un autobus a due piani, 1916. (Sopra) Un'agente della metropolitana, nel nord di Londra, il 28 dicembre 1916. Con i suoi stivali avrà sicuramente riscaldato i cuori di più di un passeggero, in una giornata così fredda e grigia…

Work for all. Men looking for work queue at the new Labour Exchange, Camberwell Green, London, February 1910. Labour exchanges were established to help casual workers find employment.

Trabajo para todos. Hombres en busca de trabajo hacen cola en la nueva Bolsa de Trabajo de Camberwell Green, Londres, en febrero de 1910. Las bolsas de trabajo se crearon para ayudar a los trabajadores temporales a encontrar empleo.

Lavoro per tutti. Disoccupati in coda al nuovo ufficio di collocamento di Camberwell Green (Londra), febbraio 1910. Questi uffici furono creati per aiutare i lavoratori saltuari a trovare un impiego.

Free for all. Factory and mill foremen select workers from a crowd of unemployed men. The system was open to much abuse, with preference being given to friends and relations and non-union workers.

Posibilidades para todos. Capataces de fábricas seleccionan trabajadores entre una multitud de hombres sin empleo. El sistema daba lugar a numerosos abusos, ya que se otorgaba preferencia a los amigos, familiares y obreros no pertenecientes a los sindicatos.

Aperto a tutti. Dei caposquadra selezionano i futuri operai tra una folla di disoccupati. Questo sistema permetteva molte irregolarità, in quanto venivano scelti di preferenza amici, parenti e lavoratori non appartenenti a sindacati.

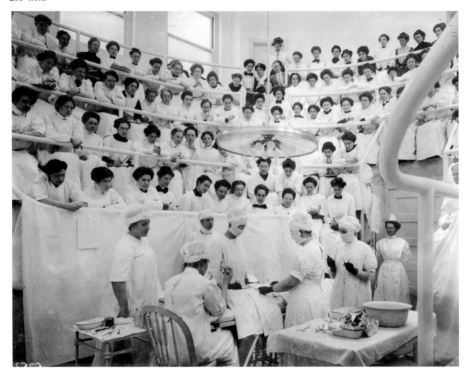

Cutting bodies. Medical students observe the dissection of a corpse at the Women's College Hospital, Philadelphia, March 1911. The provision of higher education for women was steadily advancing in the US, except in the south.

Disección de un cadáver. Un grupo de estudiantes de medicina asisten a una autopsia en el Women's College Hospital de Filadelfia, en marzo de 1911. El acceso de la mujer a la enseñanza superior se estaba generalizando en Estados Unidos, excepto en el sur.

Sezionando un corpo. Studenti di medicina assistono a un'autopsia presso la Scuola femminile di medicina di Philadelphia, marzo 1911. Negli Stati Uniti, con eccezione degli stati del Sud, l'accesso delle donne all'insegnamento superiore si generalizzò poco a poco.

Cutting coal. Women coal trimmers in the United States, May 1919.
Their days of industrial work were numbered: the men whom they had
replaced demanded their jobs back when they returned from the war.

Trabajo en la mina. Mineras en Estados Unidos, en mayo de 1919.
Sus días de trabajo industrial estaban contados: los hombres a quienes
habían sustituido durante la guerra regresaron y reclamaron sus
puestos de trabajo.

Lavoro in miniera. Carboniere negli Stati Uniti, maggio 1919.
I loro giorni erano contati: gli uomini che stavano sostituendo
avrebbero reclamato i loro posti di lavoro una volta tornati dal fronte.

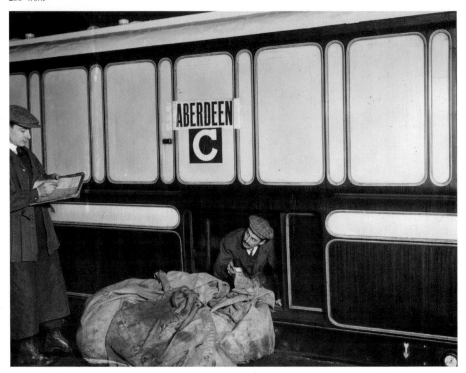

Night mail. Bags of Christmas post are loaded on to a Post Office train at London's Euston Station, bound for Aberdeen, 21 December 1912. Letter-sorting coaches first appeared on British trains in 1838.

Correo nocturno. Carga de sacos llenos de correo de Navidad en un tren en la estación londinense de Euston con destino a Aberdeen, el 21 de diciembre de 1912. Estos vagones de distribución aparecieron en los trenes británicos por primera vez en 1838.

Posta notturna. Sacchi pieni di posta natalizia su un treno postale diretto a Aberdeen, stazione di Euston (Londra) il 21 dicembre 1912. Questi vagoni postali fecero la loro comparsa nei convogli britannici per la prima volta nel 1838.

Daily grind. Clerks at work in the offices of a London bus company. The best qualifications for office work were punctuality, honesty, copperplate handwriting and a head for figures.

Trabajo cotidiano. Administrativos de una empresa de autobuses londinense realizando sus tareas. Las mejores cualidades para ser un buen oficinista eran: puntualidad, honradez, buena letra y facilidad para los números.

Routine quotidiana. Impiegati di una compagnia di autobus londinese. Per lavorare in un ufficio occorrevano le seguenti qualità: puntualità, onestà, una buona calligrafia e predisposizione per i calcoli.

British takeover, female makeover. Women employees at the Short Brothers Works in Southampton patch up the fabric on the inside of a Zeppelin gas bag, February 1919. Women were generally considered better than men at such work.

Arreglos femeninos. Empleadas de Short Brothers Works, en Southampton, remiendan la tela de un zepelín por el interior, en febrero de 1919. En general, se consideraba que las mujeres hacían este tipo de trabajo mejor que los hombres.

Prendo e rammendo. Delle dipendenti di Short Brothers Works a Southampton riparano la tela di uno zeppelin dall'interno, febbraio 1919. Generalmente, le donne erano considerate migliori degli uomini per questo genere di lavori.

Popping out for a breath of fresh air. Two of the female workers at the Short Brothers Works, February 1919. The golden age of the airship was about to begin. It lasted little more than a decade.

Un poco de aire fresco. Dos de las trabajadoras de Short Brothers Works, en febrero de 1919. Está a punto de comenzar la época dorada del dirigible, que duró poco más de una década.

Una boccata d'aria fresca. Due impiegate della Short Brothers Works, febbraio 1919. L'età d'oro del dirigibile era appena cominciata e sarebbe durata poco più di un decennio.

Mountains of tea. A team of shovellers blending 48,000lb of tea, 17 September 1916. The tea was later packed into airtight tins and despatched to British troops on the Western Front.

Montañas de té. Un equipo de hombres mezcla 22.000 kg de té ayudándose con unas palas, el 17 de septiembre de 1916. Después se envasaba el té al vacío en cajas y se enviaba a las tropas británicas destinadas al frente occidental.

Montagne di tè. Una squadra di operai muniti di pala mescolano 22.000 kg di tè, 17 settembre 1916. In seguito il tè veniva messo sotto vuoto e inviato alle truppe britanniche del fronte occidentale.

Cups of tea. Women maintenance workers at the Gas Light and Coke Company Works, Bromley-by-Bow, London, take a tea break on top of one of the gas holders, 11 June 1918.

Tazas de té. Empleadas de mantenimiento de Gas Light and Coke Company Works hacen una pausa para tomar el té sobre uno de los depósitos de gas en Bromley-by-Bow, Londres, el 11 de junio de 1918.

Tazze di tè. Dipendenti della Gas Light and Coke Company Works addette alla manutenzione fanno una pausa-tè sul tetto di uno dei gasometri della compagnia a Bromey-by-Bow (Londra), l'11 giugno 1918.

9. Leisure
Ocio
Tempo libero

Hold on to your hats! Visitors to the fairground at the Japan-British Exhibition in London enjoy the delights of the 'wibble-wobble' – an early form of dodgem, or bumper car – August 1910.

¡Cuidado con el sombrero! Unos visitantes de la feria de la Exposición Británico-Japonesa celebrada en Londres disfrutan de una versión antigua de los autos de choque, en agosto de 1910.

Tenetevi stretti i cappelli! Visitatori delle attrazioni dell'Esposizione britannico-giapponese di Londra sperimentano il brivido di un giro sul 'wibble-wobble', una versione antica dell'autoscontro, agosto 1910.

9. Leisure
Ocio
Tempo libero

There was little time for leisure with a six-day working week, but with a few shillings in your purse or pocket there was joy to be found even on a Sunday. Clerks and mill-hands, shop-girls and apprentices flocked to the country or the seaside, breathed clean air, drank a little beer, munched their pies and sandwiches and enjoyed fleeting romance on the last train or bus home. For Sunday cyclists, the roads were gloriously empty. For anglers, rivers, lakes and streams were well-stocked and unpolluted. On moors and mountains there was space to set up a tent and no need to ask permission.

If the purse or pocket held bank notes then 'leisure' meant more than just the occasional day off. The wealthy spent entire seasons in country retreats, in villas by the sea, in fine houses at the heart of great cities. There were parties, balls, shoots, concerts, regattas, hunts, amateur theatricals, tennis parties and a host of activities to delight and exhaust.

War permitting, the adventurous could pursue the pleasures of the entire planet – climbing in the Alps, excursions to the ruins of Rome and Greece, cruises to the Orient, safaris in Africa… the list was endless.

Había poco tiempo para divertirse con una semana laborable de seis días, pero bastaba con tener unos pocos chelines en el bolsillo para pasarlo bien, incluso el domingo. Empleados y obreros de fábricas, dependientas y aprendices iban al campo o a la costa a respirar aire puro, beber un poco de cerveza, comer unos bocadillos y unos pasteles, y vivir un breve romance en el viaje de regreso a casa en el último tren o autobús. Los pescadores pescaban en ríos, lagos y arroyos repletos de peces y sin contaminación. En las llanuras y las montañas, había sitio suficiente para instalar la tienda y no era necesario pedir autorización alguna.

Si la cartera rebosaba de billetes, "diversión" significaba algo más que pasar un día fuera de vez en cuando. Los ricos pasaban temporadas enteras en sus residencias de verano, en sus casas de la costa o en sus magníficas viviendas del centro de las grandes ciudades. Había fiestas, bailes, concursos de tiro, conciertos, regatas, cacerías, representaciones teatrales de aficionados, campeonatos de tenis y un sinfín de actividades más.

Y si, a pesar de todo, la guerra lo permitía, los aventureros podían disfrutar de la emoción en cualquier parte del mundo: escalada en los Alpes, excursiones a las ruinas romanas y griegas, cruceros por Oriente, safaris en África... la lista era interminable.

La settimana di sei giorni lasciava poco tempo libero. Ma anche con poche monete in tasca ci si poteva divertire, di domenica. Impiegati, operai delle filature, commesse e apprendisti correvano al mare, a respirare aria pulita, bere qualche birra, mangiare una torta o un panino e vivere una breve storia d'amore sull'ultimo treno o autobus, di ritorno a casa. I ciclisti della domenica circolavano su strade meravigliosamente deserte. I pescatori pescavano in fiumi, laghi e ruscelli non inquinati dove abbondavano i pesci. Nelle campagne e nelle colline c'era spazio sufficiente per accamparsi e senza dover chiedere il permesso.

Con il portafoglio pieno, invece, la parola "divertimento" prendeva un altro significato rispetto a un'escursione di un giorno. I ricchi passavano stagioni intere nelle loro case di campagna, nelle loro ville in riva al mare e nelle loro residenze cittadine. Organizzavano feste, balli, partite di caccia, concerti, regate, rappresentazioni teatrali e attività ricreative di ogni tipo.

E, guerra permettendo, i viaggiatori avevano l'intero pianeta a disposizione: potevano scalare le Alpi, fare escursioni tra le rovine romane e greche, crociere in Oriente e safari in Africa... la lista era infinita.

Messing about on the river. A large Kodak 'bellows' camera is about to capture the delights of punting, 1910.

Diversión en el río. Una gran cámara Kodak con fuelle está a punto de inmortalizar un agradable paseo en barca, en 1910.

Sulle rive del fiume. Una grande Kodak a soffietto pronta a ritrarre i piacevoli momenti di navigazione, 1910.

Fringe of the ocean. Two bathers on the beach at Ostend, Belgium, 1911. The one-piece bathing costume had by then been accepted in all but the most conservative of resorts.

A la orilla del mar. Dos bañistas en la playa de Ostende, Bélgica, en 1911. Por aquel entonces, el bañador de una pieza ya se aceptaba en todas partes salvo en los centros de vacaciones más conservadores.

Sulle rive dell'oceano. Due bagnanti sulla spiaggia di Ostenda (Belgio), 1911. All'epoca il costume da bagno intero era accettato ormai ovunque, eccetto nelle stazioni balneari più conservatrici.

Heart of London, heat of summer. Bold young women cool off in the Serpentine, Hyde Park, 1911. Tucking one's skirt into one's bloomers was as far as a lady could possibly go.

El calor estival llega al centro de Londres. Unas jóvenes atrevidas se refrescan en el lago Serpentine de Hyde Park, en 1911. Levantarse la falda hasta los calzones era lo máximo que podía atreverse a hacer una mujer.

Calura estiva a Londra. Due giovani temerarie si rinfrescano nella Serpentine, il lago di Hyde Park, 1911. Il massimo che poteva fare una signora era tirarsi su la gonna e infilarla nelle culotte sbuffanti.

Over-exposed. A naked swimmer is caught by the camera as he wades into the moonlit sea at Westcliff-on-Sea, Essex, during a heat wave in the summer of 1911. Such hedonistic depravity was frowned upon.

Demasiada carne. Un bañista desnudo es captado por la cámara a la luz de la luna mientras se baña en el mar en Westcliff-on-Sea, Essex, durante una ola de calor en el verano de 1911. Este tipo de actos hedonistas estaban muy mal vistos.

Sovresposizione. Un nuotatore nudo fotografato mentre sguazza nel mare rischiarato dalla luna a Westcliff-on-Sea (Essex) durante un'ondata di caldo nell'estate del 1911. Simili dimostrazioni di edonismo erano mal viste.

Overjoyed. Delighted amateur photographers focus on royal prey during a visit by Edward, Prince of Wales, to Lytham St Anne's, Lancashire, 8 September 1919. The Prince was on a tour of northern England.

Demasiada emoción. Unos fotógrafos aficionados preparan sus cámaras para lograr una instantánea del Príncipe de Gales, Eduardo, durante un viaje de este a Lytham St. Anne's, Lancashire, el 8 de septiembre de 1919. El príncipe se hallaba visitando diversas localidades del norte de Inglaterra.

Sovreccitazione. Fotografi contenti ritraggono il Principe di Galles a Lytham St Anne's (Lancashire), l'8 settembre 1919, durante una visita del principe nel Nord dell'Inghilterra.

Window shopping in the West End of London, 1912. There were no shortages
of supply – gowns, shoes, food, furnishings, toys, wines, hats, jewellery…
You could buy anything you liked, so long as you had money.

De escaparates por el West End londinense, en 1912. La oferta abundaba:
vestidos, zapatos, alimentos, muebles, juguetes, vinos, sombreros, joyas…
Se podía comprar cualquier cosa, siempre que se tuviera dinero.

Un giro per vetrine nel West End di Londra, 1912. La merce non mancava:
vestiti, scarpe, cibo, mobili, giocattoli, vini, cappelli, gioielli … Di tutto, a patto
di poterselo permettere.

The interior of the extremely popular Mudie's Lending Library, London. The library was founded in 1840 by Charles Edward Mudie, stationer, publisher and bookseller.

Interior de la popular biblioteca Mudie de Londres. La había fundado en 1840 Charles Edward Mudie, dueño de una papelería, editor y librero.

Interno della popolare biblioteca Mudie, Londra, fondata nel 1840 da Charles Edward Mudie, editore, libraio e cartolaio.

Ready, steady… cook! A group of pastrycooks take part in the piemakers' dash, 1910. The venue looks a little on the grand scale for any village fête: this is possibly the 'Office Sports Day'.

Preparados, listos… ¡a cocinar! Un grupo de reposteras participan en una carrera de habilidad, en 1910. El lugar parece algo grande para una simple fiesta de pueblo. Tal vez se trate de un "día de deportes" reservado a unos empleados.

Pronti, via… ai fornelli! Gruppo di pasticciere partecipano alla corsa delle torte, 1910. Il luogo sembra un po' troppo grande per una semplice festa di paese; forse si tratta di una giornata sportiva riservata agli impiegati.

Girls from the Greycoat Hospital School show their skills and suppleness in
a display of Swedish drill, April 1914. It was all part of the campaign to ensure
(wo)mens sana in corpore sano.

Alumnas de la Greycoat Hospital School muestran sus habilidades y su flexibilidad
durante una demostración de gimnasia sueca, en abril de 1914. Era parte de una
campaña que tenía como lema *(wo)mens sana in corpore sano.*

Le alunne della scuola di infermeria dell'ospedale di Greycoat mostrano le loro doti
ginniche e la loro agilità al quadro svedese, aprile 1914. Quest'esibizione faceva
parte del programma *(wo)mens sana in corpore sano.*

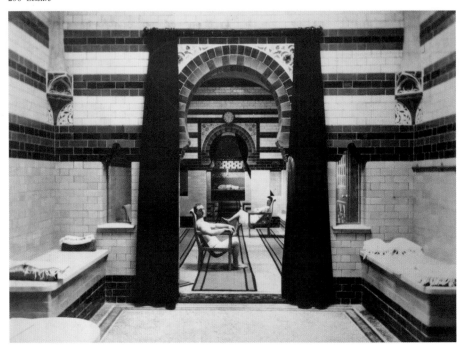

The marbled halls of the new public baths, Harrogate, Yorkshire, 1910. This grand building was not necessarily for those who could not afford a bathroom at home. It served as an informal club for the Spa's middle classes.

Salas de mármol de los nuevos baños públicos de Harrogate, Yorkshire, en 1910. Este gran edificio no estaba precisamente destinado a quienes no podían permitirse tener un baño en casa. Servía como club informal para las clases medias del balneario.

Le hall in marmo dei nuovi bagni pubblici di Harrogate (Yorkshire), 1910. Questo grande complesso non era necessariamente destinato a chi non aveva il bagno a casa per mancanza di mezzi. Serviva piuttosto come club informale per le classi medie della stazione termale.

Work-out on the waves. The gymnasium on board the Cunard liner
RMS *Franconia*, 21 February 1911. The equipment looks comparatively
modern, the clothing absurdly unsuitable.

Entrenamiento en alta mar. Gimnasio del buque de pasajeros *Franconia*,
el 21 de febrero de 1911. Los aparatos parecen relativamente modernos,
pero la indumentaria es absolutamente inadecuada.

In forma sull'oceano. La sala da ginnastica dell'RMS *Franconia* disponeva
di attrezzature relativamente moderne, ma le tenute da ginnastica
lasciano a desiderare, 21 febbraio 1911.

Skaters take to
the ice, Oxford,
30 January 1912.
Europe was still in
the middle of what
almost amounted
to a mini Ice Age.

Unos patinadores
disfrutan de su
afición en Oxford,
el 30 de enero de
1912. Europa estaba
viviendo un invierno
que muchos
comparaban con
una mini-edad de
hielo.

Delle pattinatrici sul
ghiaccio, Oxford,
30 gennaio 1912.
L'Europa era ancora
nel bel mezzo di
un inverno gelido,
quasi una mini era
glaciale.

Tobogganing down the 'New Run' at Buxton in Derbyshire's Peak District, November 1912. Most children in Europe experienced enough snow and ice to master the arts of sledging and skating.

Descenso en trineo por la "nueva pista" de Buxton, en el distrito de Peak, Derbyshire, en noviembre de 1912. Muchos niños europeos acabaron convirtiéndose en expertos del patinaje y del descenso en trineo.

Uscita in slitta sulla nuova pista di Buxton nel Peak District, Derbyshire, novembre 1912. In Europa, nevicò e gelò così tanto che tutti i bambini divennero esperti di slitta e pattinaggio.

A Guards officer and his partner waltz around a frozen pond in a London park, 7 February 1919. The scene is probably St James's Park, just across the road from Wellington Barracks.

Un oficial de la Guardia y su acompañante bailan un vals en el estanque helado de un parque londinense, el 7 de febrero de 1919. Probablemente, esta escena tuviese lugar en St. James's Park, justo enfrente del cuartel de Wellington.

Un ufficiale della Guardia e la sua compagna ballano un valzer su uno stagno ghiacciato di un parco londinese, 7 febbraio 1919. Questa scena si svolge probabilmente a St James's Park, quasi di fronte alle caserme di Wellington.

Firing from the shoulder, the hip and somewhere in
between, lady gunners blast away at pheasants in the autumn
of 1910. Where could a man find shelter from this
monstrous battalion of women?

Con el rifle apoyado en el hombro, la cintura o entre ambas
partes del cuerpo, un grupo de mujeres disfrutan cazando
faisanes en el otoño de 1910. ¿Dónde podría esconderse
un hombre de tan fiero batallón de féminas?

Col fucile appoggiato sulla spalla, sull'anca o a mezza strada,
queste signore cacciano il fagiano nell'autunno 1910. Per
qualsiasi uomo sarebbe stato impossibile sfuggire a un simile
battaglione.

A time out of war... Two attendants find shelter and
boredom at a clay pigeon shoot, 1910. Their smart white
coats make it easier for the 'shots' to spot them should
they wish for livelier game.

Una época sin guerra... Dos guardas se cobijan y descansan
en el refugio de un campo de tiro al pichón, en 1910. Sus
elegantes chaquetas blancas podían convertirles en blancos
fáciles para los amantes de una caza más emocionante.

Un momento senza spari... Due battitori trovano riparo
e noia nella capanna di un campo di tiro al piccione, 1910.
I loro eleganti abiti bianchi li rendono ben visibili, nel caso
in cui qualcuno cerchi un altro tipo di selvaggina...

10. Entertainment and the arts
Arte y espectáculos
Arte e spettacolo

Four members of the Beauty Chorus gather round the horn
microphone at Columbia Records, January 1916. The early
wax cylinder had long been replaced by the shellac disc.

Cuatro miembros del Beauty Chorus junto a un micrófono
en forma de cuerno de la compañía Columbia Records, en
enero de 1916. El cilindro de cera de los comienzos había
sido sustituido por el disco de goma laca.

Quattro membri del Beauty Chorus riuniti attorno al
microfono a forma di corno della Columbia Records,
gennaio 1916. Il cilindro in cera degli inizi era stato
sostituito da tempo da un disco in gommalacca.

10. Entertainment and the arts
Arte y espectáculos
Arte e spettacolo

The demarcation line between entertainment and art – seldom clearly defined – became distinctly fuzzy in the 1910s. The new gramophone brought music of all varieties into millions of homes, with the recorded voices of George Robey and Enrico Caruso, Dame Clara Butt and Mistinguett echoing through tenements, semis and country houses. There were grand operas, light operas, operettas and musical comedies.

The cinema produced its first masterpieces and threatened the theatre's monopoly on drama. D W Griffith established his reputation with *The Birth of a Nation* and *Intolerance* in 1915 and 1916 respectively. Erich Pommer brought post-war regard for the German film industry with *The Cabinet of Dr Caligari* in 1919.

There were great novelists and great playwrights in profusion: Mann and Hauptmann, Shaw and Synge, H G Wells and D H Lawrence, Barbusse and Proust, Wharton and Dreiser, Kafka and Joyce, and a hundred others. Poets poured the passion of anti-war hatred into the verse they scribbled on scraps of paper while in the trenches. Artists opened the eyes of the world with new concepts in sculpture and painting.

And in 1914 Edgar Rice Burroughs created Tarzan of the Apes.

La línea que separa espectáculo y arte –en ocasiones, muy borrosa– quedó todavía más difuminada en la década de 1910. El nuevo gramófono permitió descubrir los distintos estilos de música a millones de hogares. Las voces grabadas de George Robey, Enrico Caruso, Dame Clara Butt y Mistinguett resonaban en todas las casas. Había grandes óperas, óperas ligeras, operetas y comedias musicales.

El cine produjo sus primeras obras maestras y puso en peligro el monopolio dramático del teatro. D. W. Griffith confirmó su reputación con *El nacimiento de una nación* (1915) e *Intolerancia* (1916). Erich Pommer dotó de gran importancia al cine alemán de posguerra con *El gabinete del doctor Caligari* (1919).

Aparecieron muchos novelistas y dramaturgos destacados: Mann y Hauptmann, Shaw y Synge, H. G. Wells y D. H. Lawrence, Barbusse y Proust, Wharton y Dreiser, Kafka y Joyce y un centenar de escritores más. Los poetas vertían todo su odio por la guerra en poemas escritos en trozos de papel en las trincheras. Por su parte, los artistas abrieron los ojos del mundo aplicando nuevos conceptos a la escultura y la pintura.

Y en 1914 Edgar Rice Burroughs creó a Tarzán de los monos.

La linea divisoria tra arte e varietà non era mai stata chiara, ma nel primo decennio del secolo divenne ancora più vaga. Il nuovo grammofono permise a milioni di famiglie di scoprire i diversi stili di musica. Le voci di George Robey, Enrico Caruso, Dame Clara Butt e Mistinguett risuonarono nei palazzi, nelle villette, nelle case di campagna. Si ascoltavano opere, operette e commedie musicali.

Il cinema produsse i suoi primi capolavori, mettendo a repentaglio il monopolio del teatro. D. W. Griffith confermò la sua reputazione con *Nascita di una nazione* nel 1915 e *Intolleranza* nel 1916. Con *Il gabinetto del Dottor Caligari* realizzato nel 1919, Erich Pommer diede al cinema tedesco del dopoguerra il suo primo motivo di orgoglio.

Fu un decennio di grandi scrittori e drammaturghi: Mann e Hauptmann, Shaw e Synge, H. G. Wells e D. H. Lawrence, Barbusse e Proust, Wharton e Dreiser, Kafka e Joyce, e un altro centinaio. I poeti rovesciarono l'odio per la guerra in poesie i cui versi erano stati scarabocchiati su pezzi di carta in fondo alle trincee. Gli artisti aprirono gli occhi del mondo applicando nuovi concetti alla scultura e alla pittura.

Nel 1914, Edgar Rice Burroughs creò il personaggio di Tarzan.

The Russian ballerina Anna Pavlova with Laurent Mouikov in *Bacchanale*, 1913. The ballet was danced to music from *Samson et Dalila* by Saint-Saëns. Pavlova was then at the height of her fame as a dancer.

La bailarina rusa Anna Pavlova con Laurent Mouikov en *Bacchanale,* en 1913. El *ballet* estuvo acompañado por música de *Sansón y Dalila*, de Saint-Saëns. Pavlova vivía por aquel entonces su mejor momento profesional.

La ballerina russa Anna Pavlova con Laurent Mouikov in *Baccanali*, 1913. Il balletto era accompagnato da un adattamento della musica di *Sansone e Dalila* di Saint-Saëns. Anna Pavlova era al culmine della sua gloria.

Vera Fokina and
Michail Fokine in
the Ballets Russes
production of
Rimsky-Korsakov's
Sheherazade, 1910.

Vera Fokina y
Mijaíl Fokin en
la producción de
los Ballets Russes
de la obra de
Rimski-Korsakov
Scheherazade,
en 1910.

Vera Fokina e
Michail Fokine
in una produzione
dei Balletti Russi
di *Scheherazade* di
Rimsky-Korsakov,
1910.

(Opposite) Pavlova poses amid floral tributes at the Ritz Hotel, London, May 1912. (Right) Vaslav Nijinsky in *Le Spectre de la rose*, 1915.

(Página anterior) Pavlova, entre flores de admiradores, en el Hotel Ritz de Londres, en mayo de 1912. (Derecha) Vaslav Nijinsky en *El espectro de la rosa,* en 1915.

(Accanto) Anna Pavlova fotografata in mezzo agli omaggi floreali ricevuti dai suoi ammiratori al Ritz di Londra, maggio 1912. (A destra) Vaslav Nijinsky nello *Spettro della rosa*, 1915.

Pierrots and
pierrettes pose for
a publicity shot on
the open top of
a bus outside the
Drury Lane Theatre
in London's West
End, April 1915.

Pierrots y Pierrettes
posan para un
anuncio en un
autobús descubierto
frente al Drury Lane
Theatre en el West
End de Londres, en
abril de 1915.

Pierrot e Pierrette
in posa per una
pubblicità sulla
piattaforma di un
autobus davanti al
Drury Lane Theatre
nel West End di
Londra, aprile 1915.

(Opposite) Marcel Proust leaves the sound-proof flat in which
he wrote to pose outside a window, 1910. (Above) The French
novelist Colette with feline friends, 1910.

(Página anterior) Marcel Proust sale del apartamento insonorizado
en el que escribía para posar fuera junto a una ventana, en 1910.
(Arriba) La novelista francesa Colette con sus gatos, en 1910.

(Accanto) Marcel Proust lascia il suo appartamento insonorizzato
nel quale scrive per posare fuori, davanti a una finestra, 1910.
(Sopra) La scrittrice francese Colette con i suoi amici gatti, 1910.

Emilio Filippo Tommaso Marinetti, writer and founder of the Futurist movement, 1915. Marinetti glorified speed, 'dynamism' and, above all, war. In 1919 he joined the Italian Fascists.

Emilio Filippo Tommaso Marinetti, escritor y fundador del futurismo, 1915. Marinetti ensalzaba la velocidad, el "dinamismo" y, sobre todo, la guerra. En 1919 se convirtió en miembro del partido fascista italiano.

Emilio Filippo Tommaso Marinetti, scrittore e fondatore del movimento futurista, nel 1915. Marinetti glorificò la velocità, il "dinamismo" e soprattutto la guerra. Nel 1919, divenne membro del partito fascista italiano.

Luigi Russolo and his assistant Piatti prepare the noise machine
that performed Russolo's 'Futurist' symphonies, 1913. One of
them was staged at the London Coliseum in June 1914.

Luigi Russolo y su ayudante Piatti preparan la máquina de ruido
que interpretó las sinfonías "futuristas" de Russolo, en 1913.
Una de las sinfonías se representó en el London Coliseum en
junio de 1914.

Luigi Russolo e il suo assistente Piatti preparano la "macchina dei
rumori" che eseguiva le sinfonie futuriste di Russolo, 1913. Una
delle sinfonie fu eseguita al London Coliseum nel giugno del 1914.

Towards the end of his life, Auguste Renoir paints on, 1915. He was almost crippled with arthritis.

Hacia el final de su vida, en 1915, Auguste Renoir todavía pintaba. Por aquel entonces, la artritis prácticamente le había paralizado.

Ormai alla fine dei suoi giorni, Auguste Renoir dipinge ancora, 1915. L'artrite l'ha paralizzato quasi completamente.

Henri Matisse, the founder of the Fauvists, in his Paris studio, 13 May 1913. The days of poverty were now behind him.

Henri Matisse, fundador del fovismo, en su estudio de París, el 13 de mayo de 1913. Los días de pobreza ya habían quedado atrás.

Henri Matisse, il fondatore del fauvismo, nel suo studio di Parigi il 13 maggio 1913. Si è ormai lasciato alle spalle i giorni della povertà.

James Montgomery Flagg stands proudly beside his famous recruiting poster, 1918. It was based on an earlier British poster of Kitchener.

James Montgomery Flagg posa con orgullo junto a su famoso cartel a favor del alistamiento, en 1918. Estaba basado en un póster británico anterior de Kitchener.

James Montgomery Flagg posa orgoglioso accanto al suo celebre poster per la mobilitazione, 1918, ispirato a un poster precedente del britannico Kitchener.

A still from a typical anti-German MGM film of 1918. Most governments quickly realised the powerful role that cinema could play in the war of propaganda, and encouraged studios to make such films.

Escena de una típica película antialemana producida por la MGM en 1918. La mayoría de los gobiernos se dieron cuenta muy pronto de la importante función que podía desempeñar el cine en la guerra propagandística y alentaron a los estudios a producir este tipo de películas.

Scena di un tipico film antitedesco prodotto dalla MGM nel 1918. La maggior parte dei governi capirono rapidamente che il cinema poteva avere un ruolo determinante nella guerra di propaganda e incoraggiarono gli studios a realizzare film simili.

For King and Country… The American-born British sculptor Jacob Epstein in uniform, 1917.

Para el rey y para el país… El escultor británico de origen estadounidense Jacob Epstein posa en uniforme, en 1917.

Per il re e la patria… Lo scultore britannico di origine americana Jacob Epstein posa in uniforme, 1917.

For Uncle Sam
and Broadway…
The Russian-born
US composer Irving
Berlin in costume
for *Over There*,
1918.

Para el tío Sam y
para Broadway…
El compositor
estadounidense de
origen ruso Irving
Berlin, ataviado
para *Over There*,
en 1918.

Per lo zio Sam
e Broadway…
Il compositore
americano di origine
russa Irving Berlin
posa in costume
per *Over There*,
1918.

A typical scene from the early screen melodrama *The Telegrapher's Daughter*, 1914. The heroine appears doomed, but note the conveniently placed points: they should guarantee her survival.

Escena típica de uno de los primeros melodramas llevados a la pantalla, *La hija del telegrafista* (1914). La heroína parece sentenciada, pero destaca la magnífica puesta en escena: la intersección de las vías debería permitirle escapar a una muerte trágica.

Scena classica di uno dei primi melodrammi filmati, *The Telegrapher's Daughter*, del 1914. L'eroina sembra condannata, ma la messa in scena è astuta: l'intersezione delle rotaie dovrebbe salvarla.

The famous Keystone Kops, created and directed by Mack Sennett, 1913. On the left, with the telephone, is Ford Sterling. On the far right is a young Roscoe 'Fatty' Arbuckle.

Los famosos Keystone Kops, creados y dirigidos por Mack Sennett, en 1913. A la izquierda, con el teléfono, está Ford Sterling. Y a la derecha del todo se encuentra un joven Roscoe *Fatty* Arbuckle.

Le celebri Keystone Kops, create e messe in scena da Mack Sennett, 1913. A sinistra, al telefono, Ford Sterling e, a destra, il giovane Roscoe "Fatty" Arbuckle.

(Above) Giants of the early cinema on the day they formed the United Artists corporation, 17 April 1919. (From left to right) Douglas Fairbanks Snr, David Wark Griffith, Mary Pickford and Charlie Chaplin. (Opposite) Chaplin operates a movie camera, 1915.

(Arriba) Las grandes figuras de los comienzos del cine el día que crearon la United Artists Corporation, el 17 de abril de 1919. (De izquierda a derecha) Douglas Fairbanks Senior, David Wark Griffith, Mary Pickford y Charlie Chaplin. (Página siguiente) Chaplin detrás de la cámara, en 1915.

(Sopra) I giganti degli inizi del cinema fotografati il giorno della creazione di United Artists Corporation, il 17 aprile 1919. (Da sinistra a destra) Douglas Fairbanks Senior, David Wark Griffith, Mary Pickford e Charlie Chaplin. (Accanto) Chaplin dietro alla macchina da presa, 1915.

11. Fashion
Moda
Moda

A string of pearls, a Cupid's bow and perfect poise. Socialite Lady Diana Manners, daughter of the 8th Duke of Rutland, shows the general public what it takes to achieve grace and beauty, 1916.

Un collar de perlas, la boca sensual y una pose perfecta. La mundana Lady Diana Manners, hija del octavo duque de Rutland, muestra al público lo que se necesita para tener gracia y belleza, en 1916.

Un filo di perle, labbra a forma di cuore e una posa perfetta. La mondana Lady Diana Manners, figlia dell'ottavo duca di Rutland, mostra all'opinione pubblica cosa sono la grazia e la bellezza, 1916.

11. Fashion
   Moda
   Moda

No man out of uniform could hope to be called 'fashionable'. No matter how well cut the suit, how stiff the collar, how tightly-knotted the tie, what mattered was the colour of the cloth. The best to be had were the khaki of the British subaltern, the field grey of the German *Hauptmann*, or the powder blue of the French lieutenant. The most a man in civvies could hope for was a curt nod, or a frigid smile, while his brother-in-arms could successfully offer his arm to the most elegantly clad young ladies.

Women, too, took to uniforms. Nurses attained a glamour that film stars sought to emulate. It was chic to wear tunics, epaulettes, brass buttons, caps, *képis* and fur helmets; to adopt a shorter hairstyle; even to don mannish attire.

For a night of splendour, however, the fighting man home on leave wanted a taste and a sight of luxury. It was the time to dress in one's finery, to highlight perfect cheekbones, eyebrows, lips. At balls and dances and in theatres came those delicious moments when the orchestra struck up the hit melody from the latest musical comedy, life assumed its pre-war glamour, and young love stepped out...

Los hombres que no llevaban uniforme nunca podrían ir "a la moda". Daba igual el corte del traje, el almidonado del cuello o lo bien anudada que llevaran la corbata. Lo realmente importante era el color de la tela. Entre los más deseados estaba el caqui del oficial británico, el gris del capitán alemán y el azul pastel del teniente francés. Mientras que un hombre vestido de civil solo podía aspirar a un parco saludo con la cabeza o una fría sonrisa, los militares nunca eran rechazados cuando ofrecían su brazo a las damas jóvenes más elegantes.

Las mujeres también se pasaron a los uniformes. Las enfermeras tenían más *glamour* incluso que las estrellas de cine. Era muy *chic* llevar túnicas, charreteras, botones de latón, gorras, *kepis* y sombreros de piel; así como llevar el pelo corto e incluso adoptar un cierto aire masculino en el vestir.

Sin embargo, cuando el soldado volvía a casa de permiso y salía a divertirse, quería ver lujo y esplendor. Para las mujeres, era el momento de ponerse sus mejores galas y hacer destacar sus mejillas, sus cejas y sus labios perfectos. En los bailes y los teatros, se vivían esos momentos mágicos en los que la orquesta interpretaba la melodía de la comedia musical de moda y era entonces cuando la vida recuperaba su encanto de antes de la guerra y los jóvenes enamorados daban rienda suelta a sus sentimientos…

Gli uomini senza uniforme non avevano alcuna speranza di essere "alla moda". Poco importavano il taglio del completo, la rigidezza del collo o il nodo della cravatta rispetto al colore della stoffa. Tra i più quotati c'erano il kaki dell'ufficiale britannico, il grigio del comandante tedesco e il blu del luogotenente francese. Mentre un uomo in abiti civili veniva salutato a mala pena con un segno della testa o un pallido sorriso, il suo collega in uniforme poteva offrire il braccio alla signora più elegante.

Anche le donne iniziarono a portare l'uniforme. Le infermiere erano più affascinanti delle stelle del cinema. Divenne chic indossare tuniche, spalline, bottoni d'ottone, cappe, chepì e cappelli di pelliccia, optare per i capelli corti e persino vestirsi con abiti maschili.

Invece, quando il soldato in licenza usciva alla sera ricercava il gusto e il lusso. Per le donne, era l'occasione di indossare gli abiti più belli ed esibire guance, sopracciglia e labbra perfette. Ai balli, alle serate danzanti e a teatro, quando l'orchestra intonava l'aria dell'ultimo musical in voga, la vita ritrovava lo splendore di prima della guerra e sbocciavano nuovi amori…

In the first summer of peace, three little maids arrive at Buckingham Palace for a garden party, 16 July 1919. The London Season was well under way, and the maids would have to maintain the freshness of youth against a barrage of late nights.

En el primer verano de la posguerra, tres señoritas llegan a una fiesta que se celebra en el jardín del palacio de Buckingham, el 16 de julio de 1919. La temporada londinense estaba en pleno apogeo y estas señoritas debían conservar la frescura de la juventud a pesar de las muchas noches cortas.

È la prima estate di pace e queste tre damigelle vanno a un garden-party a Buckingham Palace, 16 luglio 1919. La stagione londinese è già avanzata e queste giovani dovranno mantenere la freschezza propria della loro età malgrado le molte notti movimentate.

Stepping out. The 8th Duke of Rutland leaves a private view at the Royal Academy of Art, London, May 1914. The top hat was still *de rigueur* for such events.

La salida. El octavo duque de Rutland sale de un pase privado de la Royal Academy of Art de Londres, en mayo de 1914. El sombero alto todavía era obligado en tales acontecimientos.

Uscita. L'ottavo duca di Rutland lascia una rappresentazione privata alla Royal Academy of Art, Londra, maggio 1914. Il cappello a cilindro era ancora di rigore in queste occasioni.

Edward, Prince of Wales (at the wheel), sets off with a group of friends for a meet of the beagles of Magdalen College, Oxford, 12 December 1913. The oversized flat caps were extremely fashionable.

Eduardo, príncipe de Gales (al volante), listo para acudir con un grupo de amigos a una partida de caza en el Magdalen College de Oxford, el 12 de diciembre de 1913. Por aquel entonces, las gorras grandes estaban muy de moda.

Edoardo, principe di Galles (al volante), pronto a partire con alcuni amici per una battuta di caccia al Magdalen College a Oxford, il 12 dicembre 1913. All'epoca, i cappelli oversize erano molto di moda.

Young lady-in-waiting, 1919. Bessie Wallis Spencer (later Edward's wife and Duchess of Windsor) in an elegant summer dress.

Una futura dama, 1919. Bessie Wallis Spencer (última esposa de Eduardo y duquesa de Windsor) con un elegante atuendo estival.

Una futura lady, 1919. Bessie Wallis Spencer (la futura sposa di Edoardo e duchessa di Windsor) in un elegante abito estivo.

A young woman skater performs a daring pirouette on a frozen pond in a Berlin park, 15 January 1914.

Una joven patinadora realiza una arriesgada pirueta en el estanque helado de un parque de Berlín, el 15 de enero de 1914.

Una giovane pattinatrice fa una piroetta azzardata su un laghetto ghiacciato di un parco di Berlino, il 15 gennaio 1914.

Marguerite and Frank Gill dip and glide their way through an exhibition of the Brazilian maxixe at the Criterion restaurant, London, 7 January 1914. The 'Cri' was very much in vogue at the time.

Marguerite y Frank Gill ejecutan un paso de baile durante una demostración de *maxixe* brasileño, una especie de polca, celebrada en el restaurante Criterion de Londres, el 7 de enero de 1914. El "Cri" estaba muy en boga por aquel entonces.

Marguerite e Frank Gill eseguono un passo di danza durante un'esibizione di "maxixe" brasiliano, un tipo di polka, al ristorante Criterion di Londra, il 7 gennaio 1914. Il "Cri" era molto di moda all'epoca.

A summer's day, a picnic hamper, a skiff with plenty of cushions, and a portable gramophone. The wonders of the wind-up, thanks to the Decca Company, create an afternoon of bliss, August 1919.

Un bonito día de verano, una cesta de jira, una barca llena de cojines y un gramófono portátil. Gracias a los milagros de la compañía Decca, eso era suficiente para pasar una tarde magnífica, en agosto de 1919.

In una bella giornata estiva basta un cestino da picnic, una barca piena di cuscini e un grammofono portatile per un pomeriggio di puro piacere. Grazie a Decca, agosto 1919.

Designers of sporting costumes still placed propriety above comfort. The outfit worn by Miss Kyle at Portrush, County Antrim, Ulster, in May 1911 would appear to be more suitable for ballooning than golf.

Los diseñadores de ropa de deporte se decantaban por el decoro en detrimento de la comodidad. El conjunto que lleva Miss Kyle en Portrush, en el condado de Antrim, Ulster, en mayo de 1911, parece más adecuado para ir en globo que para jugar al golf.

Gli stilisti sportivi privilegiavano ancora la decenza rispetto al confort. Il completo portato da Miss Kyle a Portrush (Contea di Antrim), Ulster, sembra più adatto a una gita in mongolfiera che a giocare a golf, maggio 1911.

Madame Reytiens of France leaps across the tennis court, comparatively unimpeded by pleated skirt, long-sleeved blouse and nifty hat, at the Queen's Club, Hurlingham, London, May 1918.

La francesa Madame Reytiens juega a tenis en la pista del Queen's Club de Hurlingham en Londres, relativamente cómoda a pesar de llevar una falda plisada, una camisa de manga larga y un bonito sombrero, en mayo de 1918.

Madame Reytiens, francese, sul campo da tennis di Queen's Club (Hurlingham) a Londra, non troppo impedita dalla gonna, la blusa a maniche lunghe e l'incredibile cappello, maggio 1918.

Even on a cold day by the grey sea on the coast of Britain in 1918,
one could be considerably more daring, though it did not do to spend
too long out of the water lest one be accused of flaunting oneself.

Incluso en un frío día junto al mar gris de la costa británica en 1918,
algunos osaban demostrar su audacia, aunque no podían estar mucho
tiempo fuera del agua si no querían ser acusados de exhibicionistas.

Anche in una giornata fredda del 1918 sulla costa britannica, in riva
a un mare grigio, uno potrebbe mostrarsi un po' più coraggioso, pur
senza rimanere troppo tempo fuori dall'acqua, per non passare per
esibizionista.

Votes for Women! Jobs for Women! Football for Women! What was the world coming to? The Harrodian Ladies Football Team parade at Barnes, 24 November 1917 – long before the present Harrods boss took over Fulham Football Club.

¡El voto para las mujeres! ¡Trabajo para las mujeres! ¡Fútbol para las mujeres! ¿Pero adónde iría a parar el mundo? El equipo de fútbol femenino de Harrod forma en Barnes, el 24 de noviembre de 1917, mucho tiempo antes de que el actual propietario de Harrods se convirtiera en presidente del club de fútbol de Fulham.

Diritto di voto per le donne! Lavoro per le donne! Il calcio per le donne! Dove andremo a finire? La squadra femminile di calcio di Harrods a Barnes, il 24 novembre 1917, molto prima che l'attuale proprietario di Harrods assuma la direzione del Fulham.

Even in the 1910s comedians dreamed of being able to make jokes about 'it's a fair cop'. Here was one of their first opportunities. Women police recruits parade in their 'civvies', 30 January 1917...

Ya en la década de 1910 los cómicos británicos empezaron a hacer chistes con la expresión "it's a fair cop" (que significa al mismo tiempo "me ha pillado" y "no está mal la policía"). La fotografía recoge una de las primeras ocasiones: nuevas reclutas de la policía forman vestidas de civil, el 30 de enero de 1917...

Già nel 1910 i comici britannici sognavano di poter scherzare sull'espressione 'it's a fair cop' ("è giusto" e "mica male la poliziotta"). Una delle prime occasioni: le nuove reclute della polizia in abiti civili, il 30 gennaio 1917...

...a couple of hours later, the same recruits parade in their uniforms. The unit was attached to a munitions factory, where most of the workforce would have been made up of women.

... un par de horas después, las mismas reclutas desfilan con uniforme. La unidad estaba asignada a una fábrica de municiones, donde la mayor parte de la mano de obra era femenina.

...e, qualche ora dopo, in uniforme. Quest'unità era in servizio presso una fabbrica di munizioni, dove la maggioranza degli agenti erano donne.

The outfits were not the smartest, but beauty rather than fashion was in the eyes of the beholders on this summer's day in 1910.

Los conjuntos no eran los más elegantes, pero para la pareja que disfrutaba de este día estival de 1910 la belleza que brillaba en sus ojos era más importante que la moda.

Esistevano tenute più eleganti, ma in questa giornata d'estate del 1910, ciò che contava di più era la bellezza e non la moda.

A young Parisienne shows off her high-collared three-quarter length coat with bell-cuffs, November 1916.

Una joven parisina muestra su abrigo tres cuartos de cuello alto y mangas acampanadas, en noviembre de 1916.

Una giovane parigina sfoggia un tre quarti con collo alto e maniche a campana, novembre 1916.

12. Transport
Transporte
Mezzi di trasporto

The robustness of the modern bicycle is tested by those who prefer not to pay to see the Hendon Aviation Meeting, 13 May 1911. It was the largest annual flying display in Britain.

Estos señores que han decidido asistir de forma gratuita a la Feria de la Aviación de Hendon ponen a prueba la solidez de las bicicletas modernas, el 12 de mayo de 1911. Se trataba del salón aeronáutico anual más importante de Gran Bretaña.

La solidità delle biciclette moderne viene messa alla prova da questi signori che hanno deciso di assistere gratuitamente al salone aeronautico di Hendon, il 13 maggio 1911. Si trattava del maggior salone aeronautico della Gran Bretagna.

12. Transport
Transporte
Mezzi di trasporto

The power and promise of the motor car, the aeroplane and the submarine were revealed. By the end of the decade, flying was sufficiently safe for regular passenger services to be initiated, for mail to travel by air from country to country. The motor car rediscovered forgotten villages and brought an end to the horse-drawn centuries.

The submarine proved its malevolent worth by sending hundreds of other vessels to graveyards at the bottom of the ocean. Claims that an unsinkable ship rode the waves were tragically disproved when the *Titanic* hit an iceberg in 1912; nonetheless, bigger ships carried heavier cargoes and more passengers at greater speeds than ever before.

Trains still brought the masses to work and took them out to play. Railway companies competed in splendour, building stations and accompanying hotels that rivalled medieval cathedrals and had far larger congregations. It was possible to steam through the Alps, to crawl across the Nullarbor Plain, to venture into the Arctic Circle, and to cross every continent on earth, save the Antarctic, by train.

La potencia y el futuro prometedor del automóvil, del avión y del submarino se pusieron de manifiesto. A finales de la década los vuelos ya eran lo bastante seguros como para que comenzaran los servicios regulares de pasajeros y se facilitara el transporte aéreo de correo de un país a otro. El automóvil permitió descubrir de nuevo pueblos olvidados y puso fin a siglos de transporte tirado por caballos.

El submarino reveló su naturaleza malévola ya que envió a cientos de barcos al fondo de los océanos. Las afirmaciones de que un barco que no podía hundirse surcaba los mares se vieron trágicamente desmentidas cuando el *Titanic* chocó con un iceberg en 1912. Pese a todo, barcos cada vez más grandes que llevaban cargamentos cada vez más pesados y transportaban cada vez a más gente navegaban a una velocidad jamás alcanzada hasta la fecha.

Los trenes seguían transportando a las masas al centro de trabajo y a los lugares de ocio. Las compañías ferroviarias competían en esplendor y construían estaciones y hoteles que recordaban a las catedrales medievales y congregaban a mucha más gente. Ya era posible subir los Alpes, cruzar la llanura australiana, aventurarse en el círculo polar ártico y atravesar en tren todos los continentes excepto la Antártida.

La potenza e il futuro brillante dell'automobile, dell'aereo e del sottomarino divennero evidenti. Alla fine del decennio, l'aereo era diventato un mezzo di trasporto abbastanza sicuro da potere essere utilizzato per il trasporto di passeggeri e l'invio di posta da un paese all'altro. Per quanto riguarda l'automobile, permise di riscoprire villaggi dimenticati e mettere fine a secoli di trasporto trainato da cavalli.

Il sottomarino rivelò una natura malvagia facendo colare a picco centinaia di navi. La leggenda di una nave inaffondabile che solcava i mari fu smentita tragicamente quando il *Titanic* urtò un iceberg nel 1912. Malgrado tutto, navi sempre più grandi trasportavano carichi sempre più pesanti e un numero sempre maggiore di passeggeri si muoveva a una velocità in costante aumento.

I treni continuavano a trasportare la massa, per lavoro e per piacere. Le società ferroviarie rivaleggiavano in splendore, con stazioni e hotel imponenti come cattedrali medievali, ma con molti più visitatori. In treno era ormai possibile attraversare le Alpi e la pianura di Nullarbor, e raggiungere il Circolo Polare e tutti i continenti del mondo, eccetto l'Antartide.

A proud and
glorious moment –
the SS *Titanic* leaves
Belfast for her sea
trials, April 1912.

Un momento de
orgullo y de gloria:
el *Titanic* zarpa de
Belfast para realizar
pruebas en el mar,
en abril de 1912.

Un momento di
gloria e orgoglio:
il *Titanic* lascia
Belfast per fare
una prova in
mare, aprile 1912.

Ned Parfett sells newspapers with details of the tragic end of the *Titanic*, 16 April 1912. Six years later he was killed on the Western Front.

Ned Parfett vende periódicos que recogen los detalles del trágico final del *Titanic*, el 16 de abril de 1912. Seis años después murió en el frente occidental.

Ned Parfett vende i giornali che riportano la tragica fine del *Titanic* il 16 aprile 1912. Sei anni più tardi, morirà sul fronte occidentale.

End of the line. Men dismantle the bodies of horse-drawn buses, May 1911. Few mourned their passing, and anyway city centres were fast becoming unsuitable for working animals.

Fin del trayecto. Un grupo de hombres desmantela "autobuses" tirados por caballos, en mayo de 1911. Algunos lamentaron la desaparición de este medio de transporte pero, en cualquier caso, los centros de las ciudades pronto pasaron a ser inadecuados para los animales de carga.

Capolinea. Questi uomini stanno smantellando degli "autobus" trainati da cavalli, maggio 1911. Pochi rimpiansero questo mezzo di trasporto, tanto più che le città erano sempre meno adatte agli animali da tiro.

Start of the day. Rows of new motor buses in the fitting shop of a bus garage, May 1911. Though no faster than their horse-drawn predecessors, they were at least cheaper to run.

Un nuevo día. Filas de flamantes autobuses motorizados estacionados en una cochera, en mayo de 1911. Aunque no eran mucho más rápidos que sus predecesores tirados por caballos, su mantenimiento resultaba más económico.

Inizio di un nuovo giorno. File di autobus a motore parcheggiate nel deposito degli autobus, maggio 1911. Anche se non erano molto più rapidi dei loro antenati trainati da cavalli, questi mezzi erano senz'altro più economici.

'The only history that is worth a tinker's damn is the history we make today' – Henry Ford. The flywheel assembly line in the new $28,000 Ford motor plant at Highland Park, Detroit, 1914.

"La única historia que merece la pena ser contada es la que construimos ahora" (Henry Ford). Cadena de montaje de volantes instalada en la nueva fábrica de Ford ubicada en Highland Park (Detroit) y valorada en 28.000 dólares, en 1914.

"La sola storia che valga la pena raccontare è quella che stiamo scrivendo oggi" – Henry Ford. Catena di montaggio di volanti installata nella nuova fabbrica di Ford a Highland Park (Detroit), costata 28.000 dollari nel 1914.

The general assembly line at Highland Park. Ford workers were among the highest paid in the United States. At this time the national average wage was $2.40 a day: Ford paid $5.00.

Conjunto de la cadena de montaje de Highland Park. Los salarios de los obreros de Ford eran de los más elevados que se pagaban en Estados Unidos. Por entonces, el salario medio nacional era de 2,40 dólares diarios y Ford pagaba 5 dólares.

La catena di montaggio di Highland Park. I salari degli operai di Ford figuravano tra quelli più elevati degli Stati Uniti. A quest'epoca, il salario medio nazionale era di 2,40 dollari al giorno, contro i 5 dollari della Ford.

Claude Grahame-White, one of the greatest British aviation pioneers,
takes off in a Farman III biplane from outside the White House on
Executive Avenue, Washington DC, 4 October 1910.

Claude Grahame-White, uno de los grandes pioneros de la aviación
británica, despega a bordo de un biplano Farman III junto a la Casa
Blanca en Executive Avenue, Washington DC, el 4 de octubre de 1910.

Claude Grahame-White, uno dei grandi pionieri dell'aviazione
britannica, decolla a bordo di un biplano Farman III all'esterno
della Casa Bianca, sull'Executive Avenue a Washington DC, il
4 ottobre 1910.

A Bristol Prier monoplane from the Bristol Flying School circles over Stonehenge, Wiltshire, in 1911. Notable landmarks such as Stonehenge were invaluable navigation aids for early pilots.

Un monoplano Bristol Prier perteneciente a la escuela de pilotos de Bristol sobrevuela Stonehenge, Wiltshire, en 1911. Puntos de referencia tan reconocibles como Stonehenge resultaban de gran ayuda para los primeros pilotos.

Un monoplano Bristol Pier appartenente alla scuola di volo di Bristol sorvola Stonehenge (Wiltshire), nel 1911. Punti di riferimento quali Stonehenge erano di gran aiuto per i piloti dell'epoca.

Stunt flyer Lincoln
Beachey in a Curtiss
biplane races against
Barney Oldfield in
his Christie, Ascot
Park, Los Angeles,
14 February 1914.

El piloto acróbata
Lincoln Beachey, a
bordo de un biplano
Curtiss compite con
Barney Oldfield
al volante de un
Christie, en Ascot
Park, Los Ángeles,
el 14 de febrero
de 1914.

Il pilota cascatore
Lincoln Beachey a
bordo di un biplano
Curtiss corre contro
Barney Oldfield al
volante di una
Christie, a Ascot
Park (Los Angeles),
il 14 febbraio 1914.

The west crossover junction of the District, Circle and Whitechapel lines, a short distance from Liverpool Street Underground station, 30 July 1912. From 1914, London's transport system was ruled by Albert Stanley, later Lord Ashfield.

Intersección oeste de las líneas District, Circle y Whitechapel, cerca de la estación subterránea de Liverpool Street, el 30 de julio de 1912. A partir de 1914, el sistema de transporte londinense fue dirigido por Albert Stanley, futuro Lord Ashfield.

Intersezione occidentale delle linee District, Circle e Whitechapel, non lontano dalla stazione del metrò di Liverpool Street, 30 luglio 1912. A partire dal 1914, la rete di trasporti londinesi fu diretta da Albert Stanley, futuro Lord Ashfield.

A down-to-earth lesson in flying for Princess Ludwig of Löwenstein-Wertheim, 12 June 1914. Sharing the dual controls with Her Highness is Mr Baumann of the Beatty Flying School.

Una lección práctica de pilotaje en tierra para la princesa Ludwig de Löwenstein-Wertheim, el 12 de junio de 1914. El Sr. Baumann, de la escuela de aviación de Beatty tiene el placer de compartir los mandos con su alteza.

Una lezione di pilotaggio "terra terra" per la principessa Ludwig di Löwenstein-Wertheim, il 12 giugno 1914. Il signor Baumann della scuola di volo di Beatty ha l'onore di dividere i comandi con Sua Altezza.

The soaring imagination of designers in the early days of flying
produced many strange-looking craft – few of which actually
managed to soar. One such was the Roshon multiplane (above)
of 1910.

La imaginación desbordante de los diseñadores de los primeros
aviones dio lugar a extraños aparatos. No obstante, pocos de ellos
lograron elevarse por los aires, como este multiplano Roshon (arriba)
de 1910.

L'immaginazione dei primi ideatori di aerei produceva strani
apparecchi. Pochi riuscivano ad alzarsi in aria, come questo Roshon
(sopra) del 1910.

A gantry of forty-four signals at Rugby, on the London and North West Railway. Rugby was a 'railway town' on the main line from London to the north of England and Scotland.

Pórtico con 44 señales en Rugby, en la línea férrea de Londres y el Noroeste. Rugby era una "ciudad ferroviaria" levantada en la línea principal que iba de Londres al norte de Inglaterra y a Escocia.

Un ponte con 44 segnali a Rugby, sulla linea Londra e Nord-Ovest. Rugby era un importante nodo ferroviario della linea che collegava Londra con il nord dell'Inghilterra e la Scozia.

13. Sport
   Deporte
   Sport

George Burdett thwarts a Liverpool attack on the Woolwich Arsenal goal, 2 September 1911. Three years later, the club dropped 'Woolwich' and became simply 'Arsenal'.

George Burdett frustra un ataque del Liverpool contra la meta del Woolwich Arsenal en un partido disputado el 2 de septiembre de 1911. Tres años después el equipo suprimió el "Woolwich " y pasó a llamare simplemente "Arsenal " .

George Burdett sventa un attacco del Liverpool che tenta di fare gol contro il Woolwich Arsenal, il 2 settembre 1911. Tre anni dopo, il club sopprime "Woolwich" per chiamarsi semplicemente "Arsenal".

13. Sport
Deporte
Sport

The era of amateur supremacy in sport was drawing to an end. Professionals carried all before them in every sport save those most jealously guarded by the gentleman player. In 1913 Jim Thorpe was stripped of the gold medals he had won in the Stockholm Olympics, when it was discovered that he had once played minor league baseball as a professional. England still managed to defeat most countries in the sports that the British had exported to the rest of the world, but her supremacy was being challenged by the Australians (cricket), the Americans (tennis, boxing and golf) and the Scots (football).

Sport was still divided into the muddy trials of strength of the working classes and the subtle contests of skill favoured by the well-to-do. Thousands stood on windswept, rain-lashed terraces roaring on their football heroes. Hundreds raised their parasols in appreciation of a telling shot on the croquet lawn. Money tended to decide which to favour.

And already there were instances of violence in sport. In May 1912 baseball star Ty Cobb was banned from playing after he climbed into a stand to pummel an abusive spectator. The 20th century had truly arrived.

La época de la supremacía del deporte aficionado tocaba a su fin. Los profesionales se abrían paso en todas las disciplinas deportivas excepto en aquellas actividades protegidas y reservadas a las personas de la alta sociedad. En 1913, Jim Thorpe fue despojado de las medallas de oro que había ganado en los Juegos Olímpicos de Estocolmo cuando se descubrió que había jugado como profesional en las ligas menores de béisbol. Inglaterra todavía lograba vencer a la mayoría de los países en aquellos deportes que había exportado al resto del mundo, pero su superioridad sería puesta en tela de juicio por austalianos (*cricket*), estadounidenses (tenis, boxeo y golf) y escoceses (fútbol).

El deporte seguía dividido en dos: los combates fangosos de fuerza para los obreros y los torneos delicados de habilidad para los ricos. Mientras que miles de almas se congregaban en bancales expuestos al viento y a la lluvia para aclamar a sus héroes del fútbol, cientos de personas se reunían en un césped de *crocket* y levantaban sus quitasoles cuando se lograba un buen golpe. Normalmente la condición económica decidía qué deporte practicaba uno.

Ya por aquel entonces había casos de violencia en el deporte. En mayo de 1912, la estrella del béisbol Ty Cobb fue sancionado por subir a una tribuna y emprenderla a golpes con un espectador que le había increpado. El siglo XX había comenzado realmente.

L'era della supremazia dello sport amatoriale stava per concludersi. I professionisti facevano capolino in tutti gli sport, eccetto in quelli gelosamente protetti dai membri dell'alta società. Nel 1913, Jim Thorpe dovette rinunciare a tutte le medaglie d'oro vinte alle Olimpiadi di Stoccolma per aver giocato come professionista in una squadra minore di baseball. L'Inghilterra riusciva ancora a vincere contro quasi tutti i paesi in cui aveva esportato i suoi sport, ma questa supremazia sarebbe stata messa presto in discussione da australiani (cricket), americani (tennis, boxe e golf) e scozzesi (calcio).

Lo sport era ancora diviso in due: da una parte le dimostrazioni di forza delle classi operaie e dall'altra i tornei di destrezza di quelle agiate. Migliaia di persone assistevano alle partite di calcio, sostenendo i loro idoli malgrado il vento e la pioggia, mentre centinaia di persone si riunivano su un campo da croquet e alzavano la punta dell'ombrello per salutare un colpo felice. Spesso erano i soldi a disposizione che facevano decidere il tipo di sport da praticare.

Già all'epoca non mancavano incidenti violenti: nel maggio del 1912, il campione di baseball Ty Cobb fu sospeso per essere salito su una tribuna e avere picchiato uno spettatore maleducato. Il XX secolo era davvero arrivato.

Jim Thorpe wins the discus stage of the Pentathlon, Stockholm, June 1912. His throw set a new world record.

Jim Thorpe gana la prueba de lanzamiento de disco del pentatlón de Estocolmo, en junio de 1912. Estableció un nuevo récord mundial.

Jim Thorpe vince la prova del lancio del disco al pentathlon di Stoccolma, giugno 1912. Il suo lancio rappresenta il nuovo record mondiale.

Mr Bryce enjoys a round of golf, 1910. The British Open was dominated in the 1910s by James Braid and Harry Vardon.

El Sr. Bryce disfruta de una partida de golf, en 1910. James Braid y Harry Vardon dominaron el Open Británico en la década de 1910.

Mister Bryce mentre gioca a golf, 1910. L'Open britannico di questa decade fu dominato da James Braid e Harry Vardon.

Jack Johnson,
World Heavyweight
Champion,
2 February 1914.
Johnson had already
fled from the States
and was living
in Europe.

Jack Johnson,
campeón del
mundo de los
pesos pesados,
el 2 de febrero de
1914. Johnson se
había marchado
de Estados Unidos
y vivía en Europa.

Jack Johnson,
campione del
mondo dei pesi
massimi, il
2 febbraio 1914.
Johnson aveva già
lasciato gli Stati
Uniti e viveva in
Europa.

Walter Mead, the
'Essex Treasure',
near the end of his
cricketing career,
1910. Mead was
a slow-medium
bowler of
impeccable length.

Walter Mead, la
"perla de Essex",
en las postrimerías
de su carrera como
jugador de *cricket*,
en 1910. Mead fue
un lanzador *slow-
medium* con una
fuerza admirable.

Walter Mead, la
"perla dell'Essex",
verso la fine della
sua carriera di
giocatore di cricket,
1910. Mead fu
un lanciatore
"slowmedium"
capace di tirare
a una distanza
notevole.

Taking a punt – Oldham Athletic v Tottenham Hotspur, 11 December 1911.
It was the first season in which goalkeepers were allowed to handle the ball
in the penalty area only.

Despeje. Oldham Athletic contra Tottenham Hotspur, el 11 de diciembre de
1911. Fue la primera temporada en que los porteros podían tocar el balón
únicamente en el área pequeña.

Smarcamento – Oldham Athletic contro Tottenham Hotspur, 11 dicembre
1911. Fu la prima stagione in cui i portieri furono autorizzati a toccare il
pallone unicamente nell'area di rigore.

Taking the plunge.
One of the
competitors in
the diving events
at the Stockholm
Olympics, 1912.

Al agua patos. Uno
de los competidores
de las pruebas de
saltos de trampolín
en las olimpiadas de
Estocolmo de 1912.

Tuffo. Uno dei
concorrenti della
prova di tuffi ai
giochi olimpici di
Stoccolma, 1912.

(Above and opposite) A brace of low bounces at the Queen's Club, Hurlingham, London.
(Above) Miss May Turner hurries forward, August 1918. The club was a centre for polo,
skittles, croquet, swimming, golf and pigeon shooting, as well as tennis.

(Arriba y página siguiente) Intercambio de golpes bajos en el Queen's Club de Hurlingham,
en Londres. (Arriba) Miss May Turner corre hacia la pelota, en agosto de 1918. El club era
un centro de polo, bolos, *croquet*, natación, golf y tiro al pichón, además de tenis.

(Sopra e accanto) Scambio di colpi bassi al Queen's Club di Hurlingham a Londra. (Sopra)
Miss May Turner avanza correndo verso il pallone, agosto 1918. Il club era un centro sportivo
che comprendeva il polo, i birilli, il croquet, il nuoto, il golf, il tiro al piccione e il tennis.

Captain de Tessier at full stretch, the Queen's Club, June 1918.
The absence of spectators suggests that this was simply a practice match
while the captain was on leave from the Front.

El capitán de Tessier se estira para golpear una pelota en el Queen's Club,
en junio de 1918. La ausencia de espectadores hace pensar que era un
partido de entrenamiento durante un permiso, lejos del frente.

Il capitano de Tessier in un allungo al Queen's Club, giugno 1918. L'assenza
di spettatori fa pensare che si tratti di una partita di allenamento durante
una licenza dal fronte.

Two scenes from the Military Athletic Sports Meeting at Merton Park, London, August 1918. (Above) Members of the Women's Auxiliary Army Corps compete in an egg and spoon race.

Dos escenas del Torneo de Deportes Atléticos Militares celebrado en Merton Park, Londres, en agosto de 1918. (Arriba) Miembros de los cuerpos de mujeres auxiliares del ejército participan en una carrera de equilibrio consistente en sujetar un huevo con una cuchara.

Due scene colte durante un torneo sportivo riservato all'esercito a Merton Park, Londra, agosto 1918. (Qui sopra) Dei membri del corpo ausiliario femminile dell'esercito partecipano a una corsa con uovo e cucchiaio.

A time out of war for a tug o' war, Merton Park, August 1918. Until its demolition in 1840, the park was the site of Merton Place, the only house that Admiral Horatio Nelson ever owned.

Sogatira en Merton Park, en agosto de 1918. En este parque se encontraba Merton Place, la única residencia que poseyó el almirante Horatio Nelson y que fue demolida en 1840.

Tiro alla corda e non al nemico, Merton Park, agosto 1918. Qui si ergeva Merton Place, l'unica casa che possedette l'ammiraglio Horatio Nelson e che fu distrutta nel 1840.

A string of thoroughbreds sets out for early morning training on English downland, 1910. In the last year of the reign of Edward VII, horse racing was very much the Sport of Kings.

Una fila de purasangres listos para el entrenamiento matutino en las tierras bajas inglesas, en 1910. En el último año del reinado de Eduardo VII, las carreras de caballos se convirtieron en deporte real.

Una fila di purosangue si dirige all'allenamento mattutino nelle terre basse inglesi, 1910. Durante l'ultimo anno del regno del re Edoardo VII le corse dei cavalli divennero uno sport regale.

A section of the crowd at the FA Cup Final, Crystal Palace, April 1914. It was the first attended by royalty, though George V had a seat to himself. Burnley beat Liverpool 1-0.

Una parte del público asistente a la final de la Copa de Inglaterra, Crystal Palace, en abril de 1914. Fue el primer partido al que asistió un monarca y, como no podía ser de otra forma, Jorge V ocupó un asiento reservado para él. El Burnley se impuso al Liverpool por 1-0.

Una parte del pubblico durante la finale della coppa d'Inghilterra al Crystal Palace, aprile 1914. Fu la prima partita con un monarca come spettatore e Giorgio V ebbe un posto d'onore. Il Burnley sconfisse il Liverpool 1 a 0.

Up and over. Horse and rider in precipitous flight at a steeplechase
meeting in Ireland, 1910. Injuries to both were more frequent in
the early part of the 20th century than today.

Salto y caída. Caballo y jinete dibujan un vuelo precipitado durante
una carrera de obstáculos en Irlanda, en 1910. Era más frecuente
que ambos saliesen heridos por aquel entonces que en la actualidad.

Un salto e a terra. Il cavallo e il suo cavaliere cadono durante uno
steeplechase in Irlanda, 1910. Era più frequente vederli ferirsi nel
XX secolo che adesso.

Up and away. W L Brock, at the controls of a Blériot monoplane, avoids the central pylon at the Hendon Air Show, London, 15 November 1913. Pilots in the early days of aviation were bold rather than conscientious spirits.

Por poco. W. L. Brock, a los mandos de un monoplano Blériot, evita la torre de alta tensión central en la Exhibición Aérea de Hendon, Londres, el 15 de noviembre de 1913. En los albores de la aviación, los pilotos mostraban más audacia que precaución.

Una sterzata e via. W. L. Brock, ai comandi del suo monoplano Blériot, evita il pilone centrale allo show aereo di Hendon a Londra, il 15 novembre 1913. I piloti degli inizi dell'aviazione erano spiriti audaci ma un po' incoscienti.

Johnny Marquis
turns his Sunbeam
over at Death Curve
during the 35th
lap of the Santa
Monica Grand
Prix, California,
16 March 1914.
Both Marquis
and his mechanic
survived.

Johnny Marquis
sufre un accidente
con su Sunbeam
al tomar la "curva
de la muerte"
durante la 35ª
vuelta del Grand
Prix de Santa
Mónica, el 16 de
marzo de 1914.
Tanto Marquis
como su mecánico
sobrevivieron.

La Sunbeam di
Johnny Marquis
si rovescia nella
"curva della morte"
durante il 35º giro
del Gran Premio
di Santa Monica
(California), il
16 marzo 1914.
Marquis e il suo
meccanico uscirono
vivi dall'incidente.

14. Children
Los más pequeños
Bambini

Bath-time for a larger than average family in a richer than average household, August 1919. This bathroom is a far cry from the old-fashioned tin bath in front of the kitchen fire.

Es la hora del baño para una familia más numerosa de lo habitual y que vivía en una casa más lujosa de lo habitual, en agosto de 1919. Esta bañera dista mucho del antiguo barreño que se ponía delante del fuego de la cocina.

È l'ora del bagno per i bambini di una famiglia più numerosa della media in una casa più confortevole della media, agosto 1919. Questa vasca da bagno è molto diversa dalla vecchia tinozza che veniva installata davanti al camino della cucina.

14. Children
Los más pequeños
Bambini

Life for children was improving. New ideas were trickling into the education systems of the West. Doctor Maria Montessori opened schools for the very young based on the principles of spontaneity of expression and freedom from restraint. The sisters McMillan established clinics that revolutionised health care for slum children. Societies for the prevention of cruelty to children were founded in the USA and many European countries.

The school curriculum was based on literacy and numeracy, with a great deal of religious instruction, and a smattering of geography and a foreign language. Both before and during the First World War, history teaching was little more than a jingristic catalogue of glorious achievements. In 1911 a group of English schoolchildren organised a strike against corporal punishment. They were lured back to school with promises of no recrimination. The promises were not kept. Diet did, however, improve. Dehydrated milk replaced the sugar and cornflour that had contributed to the high levels of infant mortality. At the same time, the birth rate declined. Whereas the average family held six children fifty years earlier, by 1910 most parents stopped at two. Life was better, but it was not yet good enough.

La vida de los niños estaba mejorando. Poco a poco se iban imponiendo nuevas ideas en los sistemas educativos occidentales. La doctora Maria Montessori abrió escuelas para niños basadas en los principios de la libre expresión y la ausencia de restricciones. Las hermanas McMillan pusieron en marcha clínicas que revolucionaron la atención sanitaria a los niños de los barrios pobres. En Estados Unidos y en muchos países europeos se fundaron asociaciones para luchar contra los malos tratos infantiles.

Los programas escolares se basaban en el aprendizaje de la escritura, la lectura y el cálculo, y se dejaba un gran espacio para la enseñanza religiosa y uno muy pequeño para la geografía y los idiomas. Hasta el final de la Primera Guerra Mundial, la enseñanza de la historia se limitaba a un inventario de logros gloriosos de la madre patria. En 1911, un grupo de escolares ingleses inició una huelga en protesta contra el castigo corporal. Volvieron a las aulas cuando les prometieron que no habría represalias, pero dicha promesa nunca se respetó. La alimentación mejoró. La leche deshidratada sustituyó al azúcar y a la fécula de maíz que habían contribuido a elevar los índices de mortalidad infantil. Al mismo tiempo, descendió la tasa de natalidad. Cincuenta años antes, cada familia tenía una media de seis hijos, pero en 1910 la mayoría de los padres paraban tras el segundo vástago. La vida era mejor, pero todavía no era lo suficientemente buena.

La vita dei bambini stava migliorando. Poco a poco, nuove teorie si imponevano nei sistemi educativi occidentali. Maria Montessori aprì scuole i cui principi si basavano sulla libera espressione e l'assenza di obblighi. Le sorelle McMillan crearono ambulatori che rivoluzionarono le cure mediche prestate ai bambini dei quartieri poveri. Associazioni di prevenzione del maltrattamento infantile furono fondate negli Stati Uniti e in numerosi paesi europei.

I programmi scolastici furono elaborati basandosi sull'apprendimento della scrittura, della lettura e della matematica, con molto spazio per l'istruzione religiosa e poco per la geografia e le lingue straniere. L'insegnamento della storia, prima e durante la Prima guerra mondiale, si riduceva a un inventario dei successi della madre patria. Nel 1911, un gruppo di scolari inglesi scioperò per protestare contro il castigo corporale. Ritornarono a scuola solo a patto di non venire puniti, ma queste promesse non vennero mantenute. L'alimentazione migliorò. Il latte in polvere sostituì lo zucchero e la farina di mais che avevano contribuito a mantenere alto il tasso di mortalità infantile. Parallelamente, il tasso di natalità diminuì. Cinquant'anni prima, ogni famiglia aveva una media di sei figli, ma nel 1910 la maggior parte dei genitori si fermava al secondo figlio. La vita era migliore, ma non ancora buona.

This may well be the same happy family depicted in the chapter opener. The date and the composition of the family are the same. The Decca wind-up gramophone denotes considerable affluence.

Es probable que esta familia sea la misma que aparece en la página inicial de este capítulo. La fecha y la composición de la familia coinciden. El gramófono Decca revela una posición económica acomodada.

È probabile che questa famiglia sia la stessa che figura all'inizio del capitolo. La data e il numero di bambini sono identici. Il grammofono Decca è la prova che si tratta di una famiglia agiata.

Pupils of Miss Morris's Academy, London, October 1912. Noël Coward recalled happy hours at such an establishment: 'I loved my dancing lessons… the whole routine of ballet dancing, for which I wore block-toed shoes…'

Alumnas de la escuela de Miss Morris, Londres, en octubre de 1912. Noël Coward rememora algunos momentos felices vividos en aquel centro: "Me encantaban las clases de baile… y toda la rutina del *ballet*, para el que me ponía mis zapatillas…".

Allievi della scuola di Miss Morris, Londra, ottobre 1912. Noël Coward ricorda i momenti gioiosi passati in questo istituto: "Adoravo le mie lezioni di danza… e tutta la routine del balletto, per il quale indossavo le mie scarpette da danza…".

The interior of an East End tenement, London, July 1912. Public housing and private philanthropy – such as the Peabody Housing Estates – were gradually replacing the worst of the slums, but there was much still to do.

Interior de una vivienda del East End de Londres, en julio de 1912. Los centros de servicios sociales y las asociaciones filantrópicas privadas –como los complejos de viviendas subvencionadas Peabody– contribuían a mejorar poco a poco a las barriadas más pobres, pero todavía quedaba mucho por hacer.

Interno di un alloggio nell'East End di Londra, luglio 1912. Le abitazioni popolari e quelle delle associazioni filantropiche private, come le città Peabody, sostituirono progressivamente le baracche più miserabili, ma restava ancora molto da fare.

A young rat-catcher checks her night's haul in the backyard, May 1916. Rats were commonplace residents of most houses in the early 20th century, and did not provoke the degree of horror that they do now.

Una joven cazadora de ratas hace balance de sus capturas nocturnas en un patio trasero, en mayo de 1916. Las ratas eran inquilinos habituales de la mayoría de las casas de principios del siglo XX y no despertaban tanta aversión como en la actualidad.

Una giovane cacciatrice di topi fa l'inventario della battuta di caccia in un cortile interno, maggio 1916. I topi erano comuni nelle case del XX secolo e non provocavano tanta ripugnanza come oggi.

The wheels of fortune. (Above) Children take to the street in a well-made
go-kart. (Opposite) Soldiers stand guard over two young children during
the civil disturbances in Berlin, December 1914.

Las ruedas de la fortuna. (Arriba) Unos niños se divierten en la calle con
un curioso utilitario. (Página siguiente) Unos soldados cuidan de dos niños
durante los altercados civiles vividos en Berlín, en diciembre de 1914.

Le ruote della fortuna. (Sopra) Dei bambini giocano per strada con una
macchina ben costruita. (Accanto) Dei soldati di guardia controllano due
bambini durante le sommosse di Berlino, 1914.

Wartime protest. A children's march in support of Prohibition, west London, 23 June 1917. The banner reads: 'We growing children must have bread & sugar.' Drink was seen as a cause of poverty.

Reivindicaciones en tiempo de guerra. Manifestación infantil a favor de la prohibición, en el barrio oeste de Londres, el 23 de junio de 1917. La pancarta reza: "Los niños que crecen tienen derecho a pan y leche". La bebida se consideraba una causa de pobreza.

Rivendicazione in tempo di guerra. Una manifestazione di bambini a favore del proibizionismo, nella parte occidentale di Londra, il 23 giugno 1917. Il cartello dice: "I bambini per crescere hanno bisogno di pane e zucchero". L'alcool era considerato una causa di povertà.

Peacetime charity. Children queue for soup at the Canterbury Music Hall, Kent. Most poor children were raised on tinned beef and tinned milk. The absence of fruit and vegetables in their diet led to world-wide outbreaks of scurvy.

Caridad en tiempo de paz. Unos niños hacen cola para conseguir un plato de sopa en el Canterbury Music Hall de Kent. Muchos niños pobres se alimentaban a base de carne de vacuno y leche enlatadas. La ausencia de frutas y de verduras en su dieta provocó epidemias de escorbuto en todo el mundo.

Carità in tempo di pace. Dei bambini fanno la coda al music-hall di Canterbury (Kent). La maggior parte dei bambini poveri veniva nutrita con manzo in scatola e latte concentrato. L'assenza di frutta e verdura nell'alimentazione provocava epidemie di scorbuto in tutto il mondo.

Flowers for the dead. Schoolgirls pay their respects to an air-raid victim, Folkestone, 29 May 1917. Though there were few such casualties in the First World War, the shock of death from the skies horrified civilians.

Flores para los difuntos. Unas escolares rinden homenaje a la víctima de un ataque aéreo, en Folkestone, el 29 de mayo de 1917. Aunque dichos ataques causaron pocas víctimas durante la Primera Guerra Mundial, la población estaba aterrada por la brutalidad de esa muerte llegada del cielo.

Fiori per un defunto. Delle scolarette rendono omaggio alla vittima di un raid aereo, il 29 maggio 1917. Malgrado il numero di vittime di questi raid durante la Prima guerra mondiale non sia stato elevato, i civili erano terrorizzati dalla morte proveniente dal cielo.

Work for the living. A young boy helps his father deliver coal, August 1919. The widespread laws limiting child labour had not yet been rigorously enforced.

Trabajo para los vivos. Un niño ayuda a su padre, repartidor de carbón, en agosto de 1919. Todavía no se aplicaban con rigor las numerosas leyes destinadas a acabar con el trabajo infantil.

Lavoro per i vivi. Un ragazzino aiuta suo padre, trasportatore di carbone, nell'agosto del 1919. Le numerose leggi sulla riduzione del lavoro infantile non venivano ancora applicate rigorosamente.

Schoolchildren contribute to the Disaster Fund in aid of the families of victims from the *Titanic* tragedy, May 1912. More than 1,500 people were drowned when the liner sank on her maiden voyage.

Unos niños contribuyen al fondo de ayuda creado para las familias de las víctimas de la tragedia del *Titanic*, en mayo de 1912. Más de 1.500 personas perecieron ahogadas cuando el barco naufragó durante su viaje inaugural.

Dei bambini contribuiscono al fondo di aiuto alle famiglie vittime della tragedia del *Titanic*, maggio 1912. Più di 1500 persone morirono nel naufragio della nave durante il suo viaggio inaugurale.

A young girl posts
a letter in one of the
first pillar boxes
to be erected with
the initials of
King George V,
26 January 1911.

Una niña deposita
una carta en uno
de los primeros
buzones instalados
con las iniciales
del rey Jorge V,
el 26 de enero de
1911.

Una ragazzina
imbuca una lettera
in una delle prime
buchette con
le iniziali del re
Giorgio V, il
26 gennaio 1911.

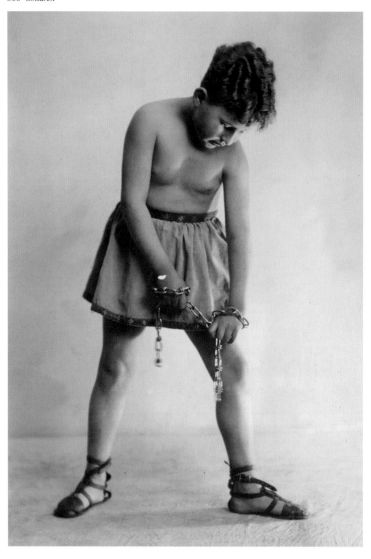

Powerful muscles.
Lichterfeld, the
10-year-old
strongman, prepares
to break his chains.

Músculos de acero.
Lichterfeld, el niño
forzudo de 10 años,
se prepara para
romper las cadenas.

Muscoli torniti.
Lichterfeld, un
ercole di 10 anni,
pronto a spezzare
le catene.

Heavy frame. Nine-year-old Maurice Pluthero of Petersham, Surrey, proudly displays his 50-inch chest.

Impresionante volumen. Maurice Pluthero, de 9 años y oriundo de Petersham, Surrey, muestra orgulloso su tórax de 127 cm.

Torace scolpito. Maurice Pluthero, 9 anni, originario di Petersham (Surrey), mostra orgogliosamente il suo busto di più di un metro di circonferenza.

A child worker in
a textile factory.
In the United States,
children as young as
six were working
thirteen-hour days,
spinning cotton.

Niña trabajando en
la industria textil.
En Estados Unidos,
niños de tan solo
6 años eran
utilizados para hilar
el algodón y hacían
jornadas laborales
de 13 horas.

Ragazzina al lavoro
in una fabbrica
tessile. Negli Stati
Uniti, dei bambini
di sei anni filavano
il cotone per tredici
ore al giorno.

So many to choose from, so little to spend. Children examine the delights of a doll stall in a Berlin street. Sixpence (2.5 pence) could buy a whole family of dolls imported from Japan.

Tantas para elegir y tan poco dinero. Unos niños miran un puesto de muñecas en una calle de Berlín. Con una moneda de seis peniques se podía comprar toda una familia de muñecas importadas de Japón.

Tanta scelta e così pochi soldi. Dei bambini ammirano una bancarella di bambole in una strada di Berlino. Con un seipence, si poteva comprare una famiglia intera di bambole giapponesi.

An unconvincing photograph of African children playing
cricket, c. 1910. Proponents of the Empire liked to see it as
a means of bringing British culture to the rest of the world.

Esta imagen trata en vano de convencer de que los niños
africanos juegan al *cricket*, hacia 1910. Los defensores del
Imperio confiaban en propagar así la cultura británica por
todo el mundo.

Questa fotografia cerca di far credere che i piccoli africani
giochino a cricket, verso il 1910. I difensori dell'Impero
speravano di propagare la cultura britannica nel mondo
intero.

Eton schoolboys set off for the College's allotments, March 1917. The 'Dig For Victory' campaign provided a welcome relief from studies and the violence of the playing fields of Eton.

Unos escolares de Eton caminan por los jardines del centro, en marzo de 1917. La campaña titulada "cavar para ganar" ofrecía una buena alternativa a los estudios y a la violencia reinante en los campos de juego de Eton.

Scolari di Eton si recano negli orti della scuola, marzo 1917. La campagna "scavare per la vittoria" offriva un'alternativa gradevole agli studi e alla violenza che regnava nei campi da gioco di Eton.

15. All human life
Cosas de la vida
Fatti della vita

Delighting in his own invention, Mr Lewis Sydney puts the Follyphone
through its musical paces, September 1912. Amazingly, the instrument
never went into mass production.

Disfrutando de su propio invento. El Sr. Lewis Sydney hace pruebas
con su Follyphone, en septiembre de 1912. Por sorprendente que parezca,
este instrumento nunca se fabricó en serie.

Entusiasta della sua invenzione Lewis Sydney mette a punto il Follyphone,
settembre 1912. Per quanto strano possa sembrare, questo strumento non
fu mai fabbricato in serie.

15. All human life
Cosas de la vida
Fatti della vita

Strange things happened in war and peace. Sergeant James Shearer claimed he had invented a machine that could diagnose wounds and detect the approach of enemy aircraft. He was court-martialled and shot for his effrontery and wasting the time of the authorities. Nurse Cavell was shot for helping her countrymen escape the clutches of the enemy. Mata Hari was shot for espionage and indecency. Roger Casement was hanged for treason. Rasputin was poisoned, shot, stabbed, clubbed and drowned, but still seemed unwilling to die.

Scott and Amundsen raced to the South Pole. The French poet Apollinaire was arrested for stealing the *Mona Lisa*. Sarah Bernhardt lost a leg. S H Schrapp of Lawrenceburg, Indiana, cracked a joke and laughed uncontrollably for twelve hours until given an electric shock. Hugo Junkers built the first all-metal plane. Argentinians danced the tango.

There were typhoons in Japan, floods in Paris and China, earthquakes in Nicaragua, forest fires in the American Midwest, and arguments about the installation of electric advertising signs in Times Square, New York City.

Se vivieron extraños acontecimientos tanto en época de guerra como de paz. El sargento James Shearer aseguraba haber inventado una máquina capaz de diagnosticar heridas y detectar la proximidad de los aviones enemigos. Su desfachatez le llevó a ser sometido a un consejo de guerra y morir ejecutado por hacer perder el tiempo a las autoridades. La enfermera Cavell fue ejecutada por ayudar a compatriotas a huir de las garras del enemigo. Mata Hari fue condenada a muerte por espionaje e indecencia. Roger Casement fue colgado por traidor. A Rasputín le envenenaron, le dispararon, le apuñalaron y le ahogaron, pero no parecía dispuesto a morir.

Scott y Amundsen hicieron una carrera hasta el Polo Sur. El poeta francés Apollinaire fue arrestado por robar la *Mona Lisa*. A Sarah Bernhardt le amputaron una pierna. S. H. Schrapp de Lawrenceburg, Indiana, contó un chiste y le entró un ataque de risa que le duró doce horas, hasta que le aplicaron una descarga eléctrica. Hugo Junkers construyó el primer avión hecho únicamente de metal. Los argentinos bailaban el tango.

Hubo tifones en Japón, inundaciones en París y en China, terremotos en Nicaragua, incendios forestales en el medio oeste de Estados Unidos y polémica en Nueva York a causa de la instalación de anuncios eléctricos en Times Square.

Strane cose successero in guerra e in pace. Il sergente James Shearer dichiarò di avere inventato una macchina capace di diagnosticare le ferite e scoprire l'avvicinarsi di aerei nemici. La sua sfrontatezza gli costò la corte marziale e l'esecuzione per aver fatto perdere tempo alle autorità. L'infermiera Cavell fu condannata a morte per aver salvato due compatrioti dalle grinfie del nemico. Mata Hari fu condannata a morte per spionaggio e indecenza. Roger Casement fu impiccato per tradimento. Rasputin fu avvelenato, ferito, accoltellato, picchiato e annegato in un fiume congelato, senza per questo morire.

Scott e Amundsen corsero fino al Polo Sud. Il poeta francese Apollinaire fu arrestato per avere rubato la Gioconda. Sarah Bernhardt perse una gamba. S. H. Schrapp di Lawrenceburg nell'Indiana (Stati Uniti) raccontò una barzelletta e rise per dodici ore prima di essere sottoposto all'elettrochoc. Hugo Junkers costruì il primo aereo interamente di metallo. Gli argentini ballarono il tango.

Ci furono tifoni in Giappone, inondazioni a Parigi e in Cina, terremoti in Nicaragua, incendi nel Middle West degli Stati Uniti e polemiche a New York sull'installazione di insegne elettriche a Times Square.

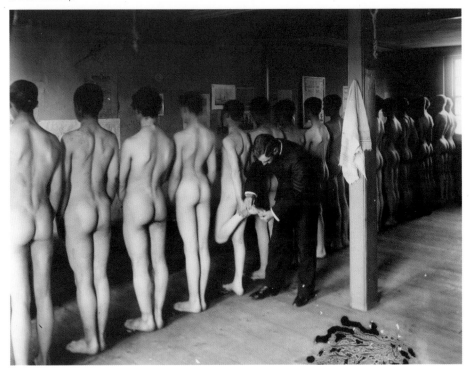

Naval recruits undergo foot examination, 1910. Few wished to kick
the enemy to death, but all branches of the services were becoming
more discerning in their selection processes.

Revisión de pies de un grupo de reclutas de la marina, en 1910.
No es que tuvieran que acabar con el enemigo de una patada
mortal, pero todos los servicios del ejército realizaban una
selección cada vez más minuciosa de los nuevos reclutas.

Reclute della marina sottoposte a un esame medico dei piedi, 1910.
Pochi pensavano di sbaragliare il nemico con un calcio letale, ma in
tutti i servizi dell'esercito la selezione stava diventando più accurata.

With remarkably little concern for their dignity, a group of men sit with newspapers on their heads to protect themselves from the sun, July 1913. Perhaps it did not occur to them to move into the shade.

Sin preocuparse por su imagen, un grupo de hombres están sentados con periódicos en la cabeza para protegerse del sol, en julio de 1913. Tal vez no se les ocurrió buscar una sombra.

Poco preoccupati per la loro dignità, questi uomini siedono con un giornale in testa per proteggersi dal sole, luglio 1913. Forse non hanno pensato di spostarsi all'ombra.

Separating the men
from the boys and the
sheep from the goats.
(Left) Workmen take
a crane to the top of
a skyscraper, 1912.
(Opposite) An animal
balancing act.

Separar a los hombres
de los niños y el grano
de la paja. (Izquierda)
Unos obreros suben
con una grúa a lo alto
de un rascacielos,
en 1912. (Página
siguiente). Número
de equilibrio animal.

Uomini, non ragazzi,
e pecore, non capre.
(A sinistra) Operai
raggiungono la cima
di un grattacielo
con una gru, 1912.
(Accanto) Una prova
di equilibrio data
dagli animali.

An owner and a competitor at the twenty-first annual Cruft's
National Dog Show, London, January 1912. The show's originator,
Charles Cruft, began his professional life selling 'dog cakes'.

Dueña y competidor participan en la vigesimoprimera exhibición
canina Cruft's National Dog Show, en enero de 1912. El creador
de la feria, Charles Cruft, comenzó su carrera profesional vendiendo
"galletas para perros".

La proprietaria di un cane partecipa alla 21ª edizione annuale del
Salone nazionale del cane, gennaio 1912. Il creatore del salone,
Charles Cruft, iniziò la sua carriera come venditore di "biscotti
per cani".

Beamish's bulldog 'Beaming Blunderbus' on parade outside the twenty-first annual Belfast Dog Show, September 1912. As a symbol of Britain, the dog almost certainly had loyalist sympathies.

Beaming Blunderbus, el bulldog del Sr. Beamish desfila en el exterior del vigesimoprimer salón canino de Belfast, en septiembre de 1912. Como símbolo de Gran Bretaña, esta raza gozaba de la simpatía de los partidarios del régimen.

Beaming Blunderbus, il bulldog di un certo Sig. Beamish, sfila all'esterno del 21° Salone del Cane a Belfast, settembre 1912. Come simbolo della Gran Bretagna, questo cane godeva delle simpatie dei lealisti.

(Above) Marisa (left) was 16 years old and 7 feet 4 inches tall.
Eighteen-year-old Asia was 26 inches tall. (Opposite) A couple from
the Rhine province who together weighed 1,031lb.

(Arriba) Marisa (izquierda), de 16 años y 2,23 m de estatura, y Asia,
de 18 años y 66 cm de estatura. (Página siguiente) Una pareja oriunda
de Renania pesa, entre los dos, 467 kg.

(Sopra) Marisa (a sinistra), 16 anni, misura 2,23 m. mentre Asia,
18 anni, misura 66 cm. (Accanto) Una coppia originaria della regione
del Rheinland pesa in totale 467 kg.

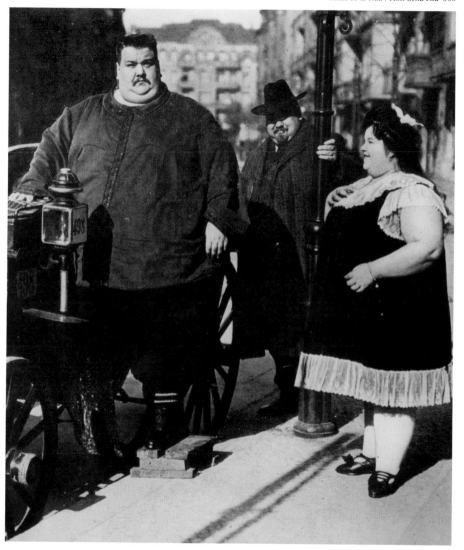

Giant Machnow and
Madame Chiquita.
The average-sized
friend was there
for reference
purposes only.

El gigante Machnow
y Madame Chiquita,
junto a un amigo
de estatura normal
que facilita las
comparaciones.

Il gigante Machnow
e Madame Chiquita,
con un amico di
statura normale
come riferimento.

Russian circus folk after the wedding of the couple in the centre, Stepney, London, 24 August 1913. There was a considerable market for displays of what were still known as 'freaks'.

Tras la boda de esta pareja (en el centro), los miembros de un circo ruso posan para la cámara en Stepney, Londres, el 24 de agosto de 1913. Lo que todavía se conocía como "monstruos" eran muy codiciados en las ferias.

Dopo il matrimonio della coppia al centro, questi membri di un circo russo posano per una foto, Stepney (Londra), il 24 agosto 1913. I cosiddetti mostri erano ancora attrazioni molto richieste.

(Opposite) Body
armour from the
First World War,
1915. (Right) Rose
Wilmot, known as
the 'ugliest woman
in London', 1919.

(Página anterior)
Armadura corporal
de la Primera Guerra
Mundial, en 1915.
(Derecha) Rose
Wilmot, conocida
como la mujer
"más fea" de
Londres, en 1919.

(Accanto) Armatura
della Prima guerra
mondiale, 1915.
(A destra) Rose
Wilmot, che passava
per essere la donna
"più brutta" di
Londra, 1919.

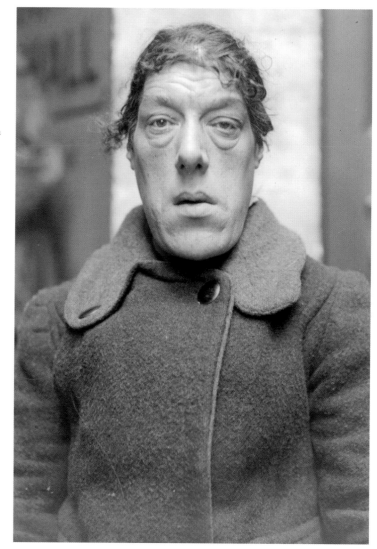

Londoners queue to read the notice posted on the railings of Buckingham Palace announcing the death of Edward VII, 6 May 1910. He had been ill for only four days, following bronchial trouble during his usual spring visit to Biarritz.

Unos londinenses hacen cola para leer el comunicado colgado en la verja de Buckingham Palace que anunciaba la muerte de Eduardo VII, el 6 de mayo de 1910. Había caído enfermo cuatro días antes, aquejado de una bronquitis que contrajo durante su habitual estancia de primavera en Biarritz.

Londinesi in coda per leggere il cartello, affisso sui cancelli di Buckingham Palace, che annuncia la morte di Edoardo VII, il 6 maggio 1910. Era stato malato solo quattro giorni; una bronchite l'aveva colpito durante l'abituale soggiorno primaverile a Biarritz.

Peers and peeresses rest their weary limbs after the Coronation of George V, 11 June 1911. The King himself recorded in his diary: 'The service in the Abbey was most beautiful, but it was a terrible ordeal...'

Pares y paresas descansan tras la coronación de Jorge V, el 11 de junio de 1911. El propio rey escribió en su diario: "La ceremonia celebrada en la abadía fue magnífica, pero resultó terriblemente agotadora... ".

I Pari del regno si riposano dopo l'incoronazione di Giorgio V, l'11 giugno 1911. Il re in persona scrisse sul suo diario: "La cerimonia nell'Abbazia fu magnifica ma che prova terribile... ".

King George V (nearest camera, on left) exchanges his crown
for a pith helmet while picnicking with members of the royal
party. The King Emperor was in India for the Grand Durbar
of 1911.

El rey Jorge V (el más próximo a la cámara, a la izquierda)
cambia su corona por un salacot durante una jira con miembros
del séquito real. El rey emperador estaba en India para participar
en el Grand Durbar de 1911.

Il re Giorgio V (il primo a sinistra) cambia la corona per un casco
coloniale durante un picnic con i membri del seguito reale. Il Re
Imperatore si trovava in India per il Grand Durbar del 1911.

In the days when only monarchs were an endangered species. The royal bag of three tigers is proudly displayed during a shoot. George V was respectfully, though inaccurately, reckoned the 'best shot in Britain'.

Por aquel entonces, solo los monarcas estaban en vías de extinción. Los tres tigres cobrados por el rey se muestran con orgullo durante una partida de caza. A Jorge V se le apodaba respetuosamente "el mejor tirador de Gran Bretaña", aunque no fuera del todo cierto.

All'epoca, solo i monarchi erano una specie in pericolo di estinzione. Il bottino della battuta di caccia reale, composto da tre tigri, viene esposto con orgoglio. Giorgio V veniva chiamato educatamente "il miglior tiratore della Gran Bretagna", anche se questo non era vero.

The Ball of the Coloured Wigs at the Countess Yelisaveta Shuvalova's palace in St Petersburg, 1914. The writing was already on the wall for the Russian aristocracy, but it was perhaps hidden by the flunkeys.

Baile de las pelucas teñidas en el palacio de la condesa Yelisaveta Schuvalova en San Petersburgo, en el año 1914. La aristocracia rusa ya tenía los días contados pero tal vez la existencia de lacayos ocultara dicha realidad.

Ballo delle parrucche colorate nel palazzo della contessa Yelisaveta Shuvalova a San Pietroburgo, 1914. La condanna a morte dell'aristocrazia russa era già stata firmata, ma forse era nascosta dalla fila di lacchè in fondo alla sala.

The interior of a slum dwelling, December 1912. Although poorly and sparsely furnished, the room appears considerably better than the worst of Britain's slums in the 1910s.

Interior de una habitación de un barrio pobre, en diciembre de 1912. Pese a la parquedad del mobiliario, parece bastante mejor que algunas viviendas de los barrios bajos de Gran Bretaña en la década de 1910.

Interno di un'abitazione in un quartiere povero, dicembre 1912. La stanza è arredata con mobili rudimentali, ma comunque meglio di una qualsiasi baracca britannica di questo decennio.

Up in flames. A balloon catches fire at an army camp in the United States,
1912. Such explosions threatened the military and commercial success of
balloons and airships throughout the thirty years of their existence.

Fuego en el cielo. Un globo se incendia en una base militar de Estados
Unidos, en 1912. Estas explosiones hacían dudar del éxito militar y
comercial de los globos y los zepelines a lo largo de sus 30 años de
existencia.

Cielo in fiamme. Un pallone si incendia in una base militare, Stati
Uniti, 1912. Queste esplosioni misero a repentaglio il successo militare
e commerciale di palloni e dirigibili durante i trent'anni della loro
esistenza.

Down in smoke.
The collapse of an
ancient Portuguese
campanile.

Nube de polvo.
Hundimiento de
un viejo campanario
portugués.

Nuvola di polvere.
Il crollo di un
antico campanile
portoghese.

The music goes round and round… A French horn player from a brass band gives his all.

Música maestro… Este intérprete de trompa, miembro de una banda de música, da lo mejor de sí mismo.

A pieni polmoni… Questo musicista francese, membro di una fanfara, usa tutto il fiato che ha.

...and it comes out here. Thomas Alva Edison listens to one of his own phonographs, 27 October 1911.

... y a disfrutar. Thomas Alva Edison escucha con atención la música que emite uno de sus fonógrafos, el 27 de octubre de 1911.

...e tutt'orecchi. Thomas Alva Edison ascolta attentamente uno dei suoi fonografi, 27 ottobre 1911.

Index

gettyimages

Over 70 million images and 30,000 hours of film footage are held by the various collections owned by Getty Images. These cover a vast number of subjects from the earliest photojournalism to current press photography, sports, social history and geography. Getty Images' conceptual imagery is renowned amongst creative end users.

www.gettyimages.com

Más de 70 millones de imágenes y 30.000 horas de secuencias filmadas forman parte de las muchas colecciones que pertenecen a Getty Images. Éstas cubren un vasto número de temas desde los principios del periodismo fotográfico hasta la actual fotografía de prensa, deportes, historia social y geografía. Las imágenes conceptuales de Getty Images tienen renombre entre sus creativos consumidores.

www.gettyimages.com

Le varie collezioni di proprietà della Getty Images comprendono oltre 70 milioni di immagini e 30.000 ore di filmati che abbracciano un ampio numero di soggetti: il giornalismo fotografico dalle origini ai giorni nostri, lo sport, la storia sociale e la geografia. Le immagini concettuali della Getty images sono rinomate fra gli utenti finali del settore creativo.

www.gettyimages.com